Breaking the Chain

breaking the chain

Dawn

With Maggie Allen

Dawn UK

Copyright © 2014, 2020 by Maggie Allen

All rights reserved. No part of this publication may be reproduced, stored in a retrieval system, or transmitted in any form or by any means, electronic, mechanical, photocopying, recording or otherwise, without prior permission of the author.

First Edition 2014
Second Edition 2020

Second Edition Published by PPR Publishing,
19 Kingswell Road, Northampton NN2 6QB

www.pprpublishing.co.uk

A CIP catalogue record for this book
is available from the British Library.

ISBN: 978 1 9164347 7 6

Printed and bound in Great Britain by Ingram Spark/
Lightning Source UK Ltd.

A polite warning

This book deals with sensitive issues which may cause some readers distress or feelings of anxiety. Explicit recollections of child sex abuse are included. Please continue at your own discretion.

If you, or someone you know, have been affected by the issues raised in this book, then Dawn would highly recommend the support these organisations provide from her own personal experience:

HAVOCA – Help for Adult Victims of Child Abuse. A non-profit making organisation based in the UK dedicated to providing help, support and information to any adult who is suffering from past childhood abuse.

NSPCC – National Society for the Prevention of Cruelty to Children
The UK's leading children's charity dedicated to protecting children from abuse and supporting families at risk.

WPH – Walsall Pregnancy Help
WPH is a charitable organisation, funded primarily by Walsall NHS Clinical Commissioning Group offering specialist pregnancy support as well as general counselling including abuse trauma support. Similar organisations will exist in your area.

You are not alone.

Foreword

By Maggie Allen, Dawn's co-author

The moment I met Dawn, it was as if we'd known each other for years, and it has been a genuine pleasure to get to know her and an honour to help her write this book.

Dawn was born and brought up in Walsall in the West Midlands, the town that became world famous for producing leather goods, an industry dating back as far as the Middle Ages. Her first memories are of the early 1970s, when Walsall was still manufacturing around half of all British-made fancy leather goods – handbags, luggage, gloves, wallets, and, of course, saddles and harnesses for the equestrian market. Dawn remembers her sister-in-law, Viv, would often bring work home from the leather factory, and the two of them would sit at the table, gluing purses and wallets together.

Unfortunately, most of Dawn's childhood memories are not so pleasant. This is because, from around the age of seven until she started secondary school, one of her brothers, Derek, much older than her, abused her dreadfully and used fear as his weapon to stop her telling anyone of her suffering.

Abuse is widespread and it keeps on happening. In far too many instances, people who have suffered abuse are left to struggle on their own and they simply cannot cope with everyday life. Our prisons are full of those who just did what they were driven to do because of their own past, their own pain – the abused child who grows up to become an abuser. And so, the evil cycle continues unbroken.

Dawn is one of the most determined people I've ever met. She has pulled herself out of her hideous past and, with her wonderful husband, Eric, they have together created a whole new life, a new family and new hope. Dawn and I both want this book to help anyone out there who hasn't been able to do yet what she has done. The first step is to understand that it is possible to change your life, to turn things around – to break the chain.

Please believe it.

Chapter one

My name is Dawn

The dictionary definition of the word 'dawn' is *'the beginning of something'*, which makes me smile because it is absolutely right. My story is about ending a life that was wrong and making a new beginning – starting a life that is just right, a calm and peaceful life, a happy life. It's about bringing to an end a life of fear, cruelty and abuse, and, because I have actually been able to create my own new beginning and say goodbye to that old life, I want to tell my story so that others will see it *is* possible to change things, to have your own new beginning. I was born in September 1968 to my parents Ron and Doris, one of the youngest of eleven children. My brothers Ronnie and Georgie are no longer with us, but Mickey, Derek, Shaun, Sean Wayne and Nigel are still around, together with sisters Pat, Brenda and Diane. They are no longer part of my life.

My husband, Eric, has a step-brother, Steve,

who is married to Pat and they have a daughter, Hayley. Pat was married previously and has a son, Craig, from that marriage. Eric's mum, Vera, originally had two children to different fathers, and when she later met Eric's dad, also called Eric, she put those two in a home and went on to have Eric, Mick, John and Julie.

Eric and I have two wonderful sons, Charlie and Harry, and we try our best to give them a life that is very far from the ones we knew before.

It's very important to me to help others, and five years ago I made a decision to do something that would enable me to offer proper help and support to anyone in need, using my own life experiences – the good ones, the bad ones, and the very ugly ones.

I decided to train to be a Counsellor.

As I walked up to the Enrolment Desk in Walsall College, I was enormously excited at the prospect of starting my *Introduction to Counselling* course, and, fingers crossed, to studying hard enough and applying myself well enough to gain the qualification that would open the door to becoming a real Counsellor. As well as the excitement, I felt nervous and apprehensive, because I've never been what you'd call academic and I was worried that I might not measure up, might not be able to handle the course work.

Making my new beginning is the one thing that has kept me sane over recent years. It has been my driving force and my saving grace, and it has allowed me to put behind me that other life, the life I used to have when I had no choice, a life that wasn't really any kind of life at all.

I hope this book will help people. I know there are so many others out there, going about their everyday existence, whose lives have been shattered by awful, dreadful things – things they had no control over. Just like my old life.

Chapter two

A childhood lost

My very earliest memory is being allowed to stay up with Mom and wait for Dad to come home. He would bring bottles of jar milk, which was proper cow's milk – thick and creamy, and the bottle had a bright, shiny gold foil top. I think this must have been for Craig and Nigel's bottles, but Mom would warm a little of it in a pan then pour it into a mug for me. I'd wait until the skin formed on the top, then I'd drink it, sitting on Dad's knee. I was certainly a real daddy's girl and this was a constant source of much teasing and tormenting from my brothers and sisters.

This was when we lived in the house in Leckie Road, Walsall. There was a verandah at the back of the house that Dad had built before he was taken ill with the heart attack in 1972, and he made a patio in the front garden, cutting the slabs and laying them to form a star shape; in the middle of the star was a circle of earth where Dad planted an apple tree. I used to love sitting out here while Mom was chatting with neighbours at the garden gate, and I'd dig in the soil around the tree. Sometimes, I'd find tiny baby birds that were pink and bald, who'd fallen out of their nest in the tree. I'd check them, over and over, to see if they were still alive, by rubbing their little necks, just like I'd seen Dad doing to the Jack Russell pups he bred. When I'd finally admit to myself that the poor things were gonners, I'd bury them in the dirt under the tree, marking each tiny grave with a cross I made out of twigs, and I'd say a little prayer for them – something I'd learned at church or Sunday school. It always made me very sad for the little creatures, but, much worse than that, I'd feel terrible that I hadn't been able to save them like Dad had saved the puppies. It made me feel I wasn't good enough…

Our house backed on to the vicarage that formed the border between Bloxwich Road and Stafford Street. I used to go down the garden and talk to the lady of the house through the wire-mesh fence. Whenever they had a garden party, she'd pass us sausages, cakes and sweets through the holes in the fence. I can't stand sausages now, just like a lot of other things that are memories from my childhood. Another very early memory is of Mom wrapping my younger brother, Nigel, in a crochet blanket – one she would have made herself from different coloured wools. She'd wrap him so tight, like a little mummy, so all you could see was his tiny face peering out. Then she'd repeat the exercise with Craig. I'd have to sit as far back on the settee as I could, so that my legs were sticking straight out in front of me, and then Mom would put Craig on my lap, she'd sit down with Nigel on hers, and we'd both start rocking backwards and forwards, holding the babies so tight they couldn't wriggle their arms out of their crochet prisons. Looking back, the poor mites must have been so hot and worn out from fighting to get loose, they'd both fall fast asleep from exhaustion!

It all seems rather cruel now… and my arms would be aching like they were going to fall off, my back would hurt so much it felt like it would break, but I wanted to be like Mom, to be proud to be able to do something she could do, instead of always being the daddy's girl. I wanted Mom to know she wasn't on her own, plus I was helping her to get 'the kids' to sleep. Sometimes, the ritual rocking back and forth wouldn't work, and I'd have the task of pushing the big blue Silver Cross pram with the two babies inside, pushing up and down, up and down, shaking and bouncing the pram as I pushed. The pram was enormous, and very heavy, and I was so small I couldn't see over the handle. It was really hard work. It's this kind of memory, when I look back, that makes me realise just how improper my upbringing was. I was more like a worker than a child in a family.

Time passed in this way and soon I was ready to start nursery school. My first day, and Mom took me to the Croft Street nursery, where the others all had their early schooling. We went into one of the classrooms, not that I knew it was a classroom – we could have been anywhere, for all I knew. Mom was talking to this lady for a while, then she tried to sneak off without me seeing her leave. As soon as I realised I'd be left there with these strangers, I ran towards Mom, but the lady pulled me back. I grabbed at Mom's legs, crying now and begging her not to go: *"Please don't leave me here!"* I screamed, because, in my head, Mom wasn't going to come back and I didn't know why she was going, why I was being deserted – I hadn't even been naughty!

My 'day one' at school is a memory I can't shake off, it was that bad. I didn't understand what was going on, why I was there, what was going to happen next... which is why, in my new life, I always explain things to my boys in as much detail as I can, so they don't have to worry about the unknown. I believe totally and absolutely that preparing people – whether they are children or adults – for anything that is going to happen to them, is vital.

By the end of that first school day, however, I was so busy playing when Mom arrived to take me home, I wasn't ready to leave! I think maybe the initial fear of being abandoned, being left with strangers, had come from some of Mom's threats that she'd shout

out when any of the kids weren't behaving themselves. One of these was, *"If you don't stop playing up, I'll have you put away!"* which was one of her particularly effective threats, because the others would suddenly stop what they were doing and everything would go quiet. In my child's mind, I must have thought that being left in this strange place was the threat turning into reality and that I was being 'put away' – if only adults would consider more how children see, hear and interpret what goes on around them, the world would be a better place.

Another of the famous threats, often used at bedtime, was Mom's attempt to get us to be quiet and go to sleep. She'd shout up the stairs, *"If you don't go to sleep, the nine o'clock hosses* [horses] *will 'ave you!"*

Once these threats had done their work and put the fear of God into us, the older ones would be encouraged to make up stories to scare me even more, because I was 'daddy's little pet', and that obviously gave them the right to make my young life a misery. While we were at the Croft Street school, Mom would fetch us home at lunchtime and we'd arrive back at the house to be fed on the minestrone soup that was boiling away merrily in a big pan on the stove. The soup was tasty enough, but it left your throat dry after every spoonful. Later, when Mom no longer collected me from school, it was left to the older ones to meet me outside my classroom, or else I'd run to the junior school to meet them. Part of my route to their school was a shiny, cobbled slope that became something of a challenge in wet weather, and almost lethal once the ice and snow came in winter, when hanging on to the wall was the only way to travel up the slope – but it was great fun sliding back down when I was going the other way!

Mom had a friend called Mrs Booker, whose son, Tony, went to the same school as me, and we'd walk together in the mornings, me and Tony racing off ahead and dashing in and out of the pathways at the back of the row of terraced houses in Croft Street. Tony always caught up with me and he'd pull my pigtails so I couldn't keep getting away in front, then we'd both start giggling. I was very close to Tony and was saddened when he passed away after suffering with leukaemia when we were in secondary school.

I was never allowed to play out in the street at such a young age, but, every now and then, I could go to a neighbour's house to play with their children. There was a black family I remember, and the mother's name was Elsie. I'd sit with their girls on the doorstep, eating sandwiches made with tomato ketchup – another of those foods I can't stand now, even just the smell of it.

Some other people I would visit were a mixed-race family, Florie and Geoff and their daughter, Tracey. She and I would play in their back garden where they had a concrete air-raid shelter, and we'd spend hours playing 'shops' until we were called in for tea. I never asked why some people had different coloured skin to my own family. It just didn't occur to me, because, even at an early age, I accepted everyone for whoever they were, not for their colour, their looks or any other reason. I've always seen the importance of what people are like on the inside, the *real* person that shows through the physical body, rather than outward appearance, and I've tried to get my boys to see that this is how we should treat people. Looks are so unimportant, and I now choose to have people around me who have *inner* beauty.

A new family came to live in Leckie Road, and this was a family who were different from us because they had no dad living with them. Mary was mom to Thomas, the older son, and two girls called Caroline and Mandy. The girls had a different father to Thomas, a chap called Bashira, and he used to come to visit them sometimes. Mandy was a very shy, timid little girl and she didn't speak at all, so I ended up helping her to learn to talk. Who would have thought that I'd be helping people in such a way at the ripe old age of five!

My dad would refer to Mary as a 'lady of the night' – whatever that meant. I assumed this was because she always went out when it was dark, when my mom would watch Thomas and the girls. Mary provided me with my first taste of chapattis.

Sometimes she would serve them with curry, sometimes she would just put jam on them. Either way, they were delicious.

Our next home was to be in Harden. It was after this move that my whole young life was to change forever, as the living nightmare began.

When we moved from Leckie Road to the house in Keats Road in 1974, we stayed friends with Mary and her family, and I saw more of the girls once they started going to the same secondary school as me. Some of the kids in school would taunt Caroline about her mother being a 'lady of the night' and, by now, I knew what this meant. I wasn't going to let anyone say those things while I was around: I felt very protective towards Caroline and I knew what it felt like to be teased and taunted. More than that, I understood what it was like to know you were different from other people – even though nobody knew I was different, or why that was.

> I was different because I was being abused by my own brother, but nobody could see it and there was no way I was going to tell. It was my dreadful secret... because of fear.
>
> Before the move to Keats Road, my childhood had been relatively happy, but, looking back, I could see signs that my family weren't all they appeared to be. Strange things, odd things, things that nobody else seemed to consider at all abnormal, but they made me feel uncomfortable – even when I didn't know why that was.

Something that had happened before we moved left me feeling I was being punished for something I'd had no control over, and certainly hadn't caused. Brenda had taken me, Diane and Diane's friend, Susan, walking along the curly wurly canal bridge – so called because the bridge followed the curves of the canal's route. Suddenly, Diane and Susan started arguing about a fish, for some reason. The next thing I knew, they were both in the murky water and they were really struggling and panicking. Brenda was desperately trying to pull Susan out and Diane was sinking further down. I was terrified and just stood there, unable to move or do anything. Then, like angels sent to save the day, a mustard coloured camper van pulled up and a couple clambered out and rushed over to help the girls out of the water. Then, they very kindly wrapped the soaking wet girls in blankets and drove us all home to Leckie Road. I remember the van's radio was playing Donnie Osmond singing *"Someone help me, help me, help me please, it's the answer from up above"* and I'll never forget that song because I had just nearly witnessed someone's death and that leaves a scar, a memory that doesn't go. As well as that, and in stark contrast to the black side of the event we'd just lived through, those words in the song did make it seem funny in a sort of strange way. Brenda and I walked into our house to find Diane telling Mom what had happened. Somehow, Diane and Susan were given jelly and ice cream and I was sent straight to bed. I didn't understand why.

One thing that used to happen regularly that I absolutely hated, was the boys would twirl blankets round until they made a sort of rope, then they'd carry the girls around with the blanket between their legs and they'd chant *"Carry my crunchie munchie"*, which I later found out meant their private parts. They would put me in a blanket, as if I was in a big sling, and they wouldn't let me out, even when I was really struggling to breathe.

We hadn't been in Keats Road long before Father Curtain from the Dartmouth Avenue Catholic church came to call, to arrange Sunday school and to welcome us into the church community. I loved the church… the quiet, the peaceful atmosphere, and the singing. And a strong feeling of kindness.

Our new next-door neighbour was Mr Hill, a kindly old gent who had painted the whole of his house in powder blue and white – even the fence and the workshop-cum-garage down the back garden, where the magic could be found.

One day, Mr Hill produced a wooden doll's pushchair that he'd made for me in his workshop – and he'd painted it powder blue! I would spend hours in his garden with my new doll's pushchair, walking up and down, up and down. On Sundays, Diane and I would be given the job of going to the local shops in Coalpool to fetch the Sunday papers and the veg for dinner, and very soon we started getting Mr Hill's Sunday papers as well. Before long Diane started sneaking money from the change and she'd threaten me not to tell on her. By the time we discussed it, I'd already been watching her doing it for weeks. I wouldn't have said anything to anyone because I was scared: Diane always had a real nasty streak that only got worse as she grew older. She once made me hang on a girl's pigtails in the street, nearly ripping the poor girl's hair out by the roots, but I was too scared not to do as she told me, scared to refuse because I knew it would be far worse for me if I defied her. The girl's mother came round and complained to Mom, and Diane stood by as Mom slapped me round the legs. I couldn't win. I used to think to myself, *"When I do things, I get into trouble, and when I don't do things, I still get into trouble. It's so unfair"*.

One morning, Dad had gone round next door to check on Mr Hill and he found him slumped behind the door. An ambulance came and took him away and he never came back. I missed him. Whenever I asked where he was, I was just told he wouldn't be coming back – no real explanation. I knew nothing of what had happened until Diane started teasing me about him being dead, at which I was devastated, really dreadfully upset. I felt I wanted to go with him so I could get away. I would no longer be able to escape to his garden to watch him working away in his workshop, which had become my means of escape from Derek for a few hours. That day I learned Mr Hill had died, I felt a part of me died with him.

After a while, Mr Hill's relatives arrived at his

house and they were letting everyone come in from the street and take away anything they wanted because he was gone. People descended like a swarm of bees... in that moment, it was as if Mr Hill had never existed. He was a lovely man and, to me, he was like the dad I used to have, when I had been close to my dad: after we moved to Keats Road, I started to lose Dad because of his illness and because I was going more and more into myself to hide away, and because I didn't feel part of anything around me. As a child, I suppose I expected my dad to be there, to be strong for me, to protect me, and I couldn't understand why he wasn't. But with Mr Hill, I had felt protected and safe.

My dad bought a new garden shed that he was going to keep his pigeons in, once it was built in the back garden. When the wooden sections were delivered, they were left for some time leaning against the fence that joined Mr Hill's now empty house. I was such a tomboy in those days and I used to climb up the shed sections because they were like wooden ladders – it was just too tempting! The inevitable happened and one day, during my shed mountaineering expedition, I fell off and landed badly on my arm in a pile of wood – not a soft landing, by any means. I ran, screaming, into the house to Mom, holding my arm as if it was going to fall off. Mom wrapped the injured limb up to keep it warm and protected, and I stayed quietly in the house that evening, keeping close to Mom.

Later, the local Big Red grocery van arrived outside our house – one of the many stops on its round – and Mom went out to buy something. I ran after her to ask for some Polo mints, because they were my favourites, but I tripped and fell on the concrete driveway, again screaming in agony to Mom. Mom took one of her old silk headscarves and made it into a makeshift sling, which she knew very well how to do because she'd been a nurse in her earlier life. I was then sent to bed, wearing the sling, but I was in such a lot of pain, Mom got my brother, Mickey, to take me to the General Hospital on Wednesbury Road, and we went on Mickey's pushbike with me sitting on the handlebar. At the hospital, a nurse had a look at my injury and then went out of the room. Mickey made the most of this opportunity, telling me she'd gone to fetch a saw to cut my arm off. By the time she came back, I was crying hysterically and, when she asked what the matter was, between the sobbing and choking, I told her I was terrified of having my arm cut off, like Mickey had told me. Of course, he denied saying that.

The nurse calmed me down and explained that my arm wouldn't be cut off, and that it was broken. She put some bandage in a bowl of hot water and began wrapping it round my arm; after a while, it started to harden and feel quite strange. A couple of days later, it wasn't strange – it was to be my weapon if I needed it. Mickey would certainly be on the receiving end of my new plaster cast if he started anything. Quite often, he'd be left in charge, to 'look after' us girls while Mom was visiting Dad in hospital, and he was always tormenting us, dragging us by our ponytails and bashing our heads on the door until we cried and begged for mercy. Sometimes, he'd climb the drainpipe outside our bedroom and knock on the window, wearing a really scary rubber mask. He always had to take things way too far. For a while, I saw him as an evil person. Now... now I don't see him as anything. To me, he is no-one.

Dad's visits to the hospital became more and more frequent. So many times we'd get home from school, or wake up in the middle of the night, to find Mom rushing about to take Dad in, or else she'd be getting ready to go and visit him if he was already in there. His health was really bad since having the massive heart attack in 1972.

> Dad was found in a collapsed state in Dartmouth Avenue – passers-by wouldn't go to help him because they thought he was drunk. He had actually suffered a massive heart attack. In those days, heart conditions weren't really understood as they are today, and so the priest was called in to give Dad his last rites. Craig had just been born, the first grandchild, so Pat took Craig to see Dad in hospital and that must have cheered him, made him feel better, and, as Mom always said, it brought him back from the brink of death.

> *Another revelation that came to me later in life was to discover that Dartmouth Avenue was where Dad's mistress lived at the time.*

I was filled with fear and dread every time Mom was busy with Dad, because I knew there would be more of the abuse from Derek, with no parents around to see what was going on, and no-one for me to turn to.

Among all of the chaos at home, there were little spells of relief for me, when I was granted some escape from the madness, from Derek, from the bullying, and from the constant worry that Mom would have to disappear again, leaving me vulnerable and unprotected. My older brother, Ron – or Ronnie, as we called him – had married his girlfriend, Viv, and I was bridesmaid at their wedding. I always got on really well with Ronnie and sometimes he'd take me to stay with him and Viv in their little terraced house by the bakery in Raleigh Street.

Their kitchen had wooden panelling on the wall and there was a proper dining table to eat at. In the living room, there was a little coffee table made of teak-coloured Formica, and alcoves either side of the fireplace where Ronnie had fitted wooden units that he built himself, where his record player speakers were housed. This room was cosy, comfortable, and very quiet. I'd walk down the road with Viv to buy fresh bread and, now they had a little girl of their own, I had someone to play with and Viv would take the two of us to the park. This was like I knew a proper family should be, with time for play and having fun together.

I loved being with Ronnie and Viv for lots of reasons, but mainly because I felt safe. Here, I could get a good night's sleep, I could wake up in the new day and play in a garden that wasn't fenced high all around like a prison. I didn't have to sneak about and hide, always keeping to myself, I didn't have to be worried or scared. Viv would bring work home and she'd let me help her, gluing leather purses and wallets together. I could talk, ask questions, and I could even stay up to watch Woody Woodpecker on the telly.

One time, Viv took me, Shaun and Diane to Reedswood Park, where there was a swimming pool and a grassy picnic area. It was a lovely hot day and we sat together, eating the sandwiches Viv had made with egg, cheese and onion. Later that night, back at home, Shaun was very sick and couldn't stop vomiting. Mom said it must have been sunstroke but Shaun insisted it was the sandwiches. You couldn't mention egg, cheese and onion ever again without making him feel ill and we laugh about it to this day, but Shaun still can't find it funny.

Viv would let me watch her in the kitchen, getting a dinner of faggots and chips ready for Ronnie coming home from work. That was different for me because Dad had never worked for all of my life, because of his heart.

It was all so nice, so 'normal', at Ronnie and Viv's. I felt safe, and loved – I felt happy. I could be a child for a few days at a time, but it was always too short-lived and I'd have to go back home ready to start school again. As if there wasn't enough of us in the house, we had this lodger – a strange chap called Reggie who came to stay with us because he had nowhere to live. He used to work on the newspaper stands, selling the local paper.

> *It was only recently, after Mom came to live with us, that I found out much more about Reggie. One time when Sean Wayne visited Mom and they were talking about Derek, calling him the 'kiddy fiddler' again, I overheard Sean Wayne say "I knew he was a strange 'un, 'cos he was always visiting Reggie and Alfie [Reggie's partner]. Alfie got done for messing with kids and Reggie went to nick for interfering with Mickey." I couldn't believe what I was hearing – why would Mom and Dad allow this person, someone who had already abused their own son, come to live with our family? Especially Mom, knowing what she had suffered when she, herself, was sexually abused by her own father. I couldn't stop myself asking Mom why, but she just said "Your dad said he'd done his time for it and so he could move in." This was unbelievable! I would do anything on earth to protect my children, I'd walk over hot coals if it meant they were kept safe, but*

> *my own parents could put all their children in such danger — including one child who they knew had already been abused by this same person! This made me so angry and upset, I couldn't speak to Mom, but then I realised that she was a victim herself — of Dad's controlling nature and of the abuse she suffered as a child. She has never been able to accept what happened to her, so she can't deal with any of this. It would be cruel to force the issue.*

The house had four bedrooms upstairs: one for Sean Wayne and Reggie the lodger, one for Mom and Nigel, Derek and Mickey in another, and the big room at the front of the house was the one I shared with Diane, Craig, Shaun, Brenda and Pat (whenever she came back home after the most recent break-up with one boyfriend or another). Our dad was very old-fashioned and boyfriends weren't allowed at the house until there was a marriage. Dad's bedroom was downstairs so he didn't have to use the stairs.

Derek would come into the big bedroom, obviously not at all concerned about the other kids being there or maybe one of them waking up, and he'd pluck me out of the bed, take me downstairs and put me on the settee. Once Mom and Dad were at the hospital, Derek knew there would be nobody downstairs, so he could do whatever he wanted. I had no-one to turn to, no-one to help me, and no choice. The kids all believed the house was haunted, so they wouldn't even think of venturing downstairs in the night.

I would sit where he put me, frozen with fear as he loomed over me and started touching and mauling, doing those horrible things with his fingers and his tongue, and I would be consumed with every feeling that was bad, painful, disgusting.

Sometimes, he'd put me on the landing on the stairs, and his hands would be everywhere, his fingers inside me, pushing and probing, hurting me so much. But I couldn't cry out, I was too afraid of more pain, more sickening disgust. In my head, I was screaming and screaming, but no-one could hear except me.

I always wondered why none of the others ever came to save me, to stop Derek doing these horrible things to me, but none of them ever did. I think now, if I was that frozen with fear, maybe they were, too. Maybe they did know what was happening but they were just as scared as me, so they couldn't help me. At the time, when I was that little girl being so callously and harshly abused, I couldn't understand why nobody stopped him taking me out of the bed, especially as I shared the room with so many of the others.

And so I'd sit, unable to move or speak, with the screaming inside – screaming with the fear, the physical pain, with the child's knowledge that, whatever this was, it was so very wrong. But I had no voice to say so. My whole being was paralysed, shut down by fear.

It wasn't long before Derek began to take more control in the house, with Mom and Dad away so much, or when Dad was in hospital and Mom would be out shopping, or, even when Dad's health improved later and he would go out for a drink on his own.

> *I was to discover much later that Dad wasn't only drinking when he went out. He was having an affair with someone called Doreen and she had two children by him – two girls. One of these girls now has a son called John and, without me knowing who he was at the time, he was recommended to me when Eric and I needed central heating installing at our house. He was in my living room fitting the new gas fire when Shaun came in and said to Mom "You know who this is, don't you?" Mom replied "Yes, I do, and I don't want to know about him."*
>
> *Yet another skeleton coming out of the closet, and another thing poor Mom just couldn't face or talk about. I spoke to Hayley about this and she told me dad used to take her visiting to Doreen's with him when she was little, and she knew all about the family. I must have been oblivious.*

Derek even took possession of the back garden and created his own veg patch opposite Dad's pigeon shed. He kept chickens and even had two wild geese running about in there.

Dad's tool shed was a few feet from the back door and the coal shed was to the right, opposite the garden gate, then a pathway ran along the side of the house where one of the dog runs was, and a path leading round to the front of the house. The front door was on the side of the house. Derek's final project in claiming possession of the entire garden and surrounding area was to build a fence out of wooden planks and green fence wire, that seemed as tall as the house. The finishing touch was a huge gate that Derek always kept padlocked.

The only time it was safe to venture down the back garden was when Derek was at work. I had to climb the fence and walk along, down the side of it to keep out of the way of the nasty pecking geese that were always running around free, then I could reach the dog run that crossed the whole width of the garden. This was my sanctuary, the place where I escaped into a different world for a little while, a world where there was just me and Rex, a scruffy black and brown mongrel who let me cuddle him and kiss him. He didn't ask for anything more from me and he gave me his affection in return. I reckoned he was as lonely as me, stuck down that garden all on his own and chained up all the time. He was my angel and he brought happiness into my miserable existence. My chains were invisible, but they held me and weighed me down, just the same as Rex. I loved this time, away from everyone else, just me and my scruffy, wet-nosed angel.

There was something in the garden that I hated and the very sight of it filled me with dread. This was the dirty old yellow kitchen cupboard with the drop-down worktop, discarded from its kitchen duties long ago and now a store cupboard for Derek's chicken feed.

Derek would lift me up and put me on the worktop, and there I'd sit, terrified and unable to move or speak, with my pants down round my ankles, and he'd do those things to me with his fingers and then his tongue – things I was becoming immune to. Immune to the pain, the discomfort, the fear, the sick choking feeling, the feeling that nobody else cared what was happening to me. I was numb. I kept asking myself why did nobody ever see him doing these things? We were completely overlooked by other houses, and someone must have seen, so why couldn't they stop it? I could never understand.

> *With the passing of the years, I came to believe that perhaps people did see, did know what was going on, but they didn't want to get involved, to interfere. Maybe they were afraid of what would happen to them if they did. I feel very strongly these days about child protection and saving children from abuse, and I want to shout from the rooftops that we need solid guidelines and much more education about these things. That would, at least, be a starting point to help more children avoid abuse – it's no use just talking about it and then not taking any action.*

The pigeon shed was another of Derek's favourite places, where he obviously felt even more confident, once he'd locked us inside, out of view of everyone. He'd pick up the old enamel bucket that was used for corn for the pigeons, and he'd stand it on the shed floor upside down then make me stand on it, where I'd have to keep my balance while he was putting his hands everywhere, his fingers pushing inside my innocent child's body, then his tongue, and he'd put his fingers in my bum, pushing and prodding. The pain of this would take over my whole being; what he was doing made me so sore and I had tears rolling down my face as I watched this little girl being abused by her brother, not realising it was me any longer because, somehow, I was now able to remove myself from the experience and just watch until it was over again for a while.

I was constantly under threat to keep quiet about the abuse, and these threats worked very well because I knew Mom was under a lot of worry and stress over Dad's health, plus Dad was very controlling with her, making her prove she'd been to the shops when she said that's where she'd been, by showing him the till receipts. This was obviously the action of a guilty man, a man who was being unfaithful to his wife, although I didn't know that at the time. Derek, of course, wangled himself into a position of control by carrying tales to Dad if Mom was a few minutes late back from shopping, so poor Mom was being controlled by them both – and in fear of them both.

I also worried that, if Dad was to die, then Derek was now in such a position of self-appointed power in the house that anything would be possible – it didn't bear thinking about. And so, I kept quiet, just like I'd been told to.

> *In my 'new life', I purposely won't conform if Eric asks me to be home for a certain time – I'll deliberately be late! Eric knows this and, even though it's frustrating for him, we do laugh about it and he tells me I'm dead stubborn, which is really an understatement! My friend, Lisa, once gave me a key ring that was a stern-faced bunny rabbit with the words 'I JUST WON'T LISTEN!' I thought that was funny.*

Dad was now on the waiting list to have a heart transplant and his health was worse than ever. This meant the older kids were left to look after us younger ones more and more. I was going to Harden Infants by this time, and, one day when Brenda was supposed to take me to school, we got as far as the school gates but she told me to wait there and she went off somewhere. When she came back, she told me the school was being closed so I would be going with her. We went walking down to the canal, over Coalpool bridge and, just as we were joining the canal towpath, I suddenly caught sight of Pat on the top deck of a bus going past. She was waving at us, or so I thought (as it turned out, she was actually shaking her fist). Of course, I waved back to her and carried on walking with Brenda along the canal side. Where Brenda took me, I had no idea then and I still don't really know to this day. I remember sitting on the floor underneath a big snooker table and playing games with some little brown-skinned boys, while Brenda went into another room with a group of men, She was gone for ages – it must have been quite a long time because I was fed pop, sweets and even sandwiches before she came back and took me home for tea.

Brenda told me to say I'd been in school and that she'd collected me from there, otherwise Mom wouldn't let me go with her again if she knew the truth, and, after all, I did get the pop and sweets. I never had a chance to tell the lie, because Pat was there. She had seen me earlier and had told Mom and Dad, so when she asked me where I'd been, in her loud, bullying way, I told her the truth. I used to call her – behind her back, of course – Big Loud Mouth, because she was always shouting and demanding in an incredibly harsh voice that made my head hurt, and I was really scared of her.

Brenda was duly stripped of all her clothes and sent to bed. This was so she couldn't take off again out of the bedroom window and climb down the old cast-iron drainpipe to get away. Not without any clothes. She was always running off from home and once even made the news headlines when she was discovered in a brothel in Walsall — at the age of fourteen!

> *As I write this, my friend, Lisa, has just had her fortieth birthday and I was at her party last Friday evening, at a pub called the Navigation Inn. When I walked into the room where the buffet was laid out, I had the strangest feeling of familiarity, but had no idea why. I would swear I had never been in this pub ever before in my life, but I was standing in the very same room where, all those years ago, I'd been playing under a snooker table.*

There was another occasion when Brenda took me, along with my brother, Shaun, and a friend called William (who is sadly no longer with us) to Walsall Arboretum, where she left the three of us playing with her make-up bag while she went off with some men. I didn't know who they were. This time, she didn't come back for us.

We'd never been out on our own before, so the boys had to try their hardest to remember which way we had come so we could retrace our steps and find our way home. When I realised Brenda wasn't coming to fetch us, I was terrified we were lost and wouldn't ever get back home. I started thinking I would never see my Mom again and I got really upset. Shaun and William must have been scared, too, but they were brilliant and managed somehow to get us all home safe and sound. We followed an old railway track up through Coalpool cemetery to the canal towpath, and eventually arrived back at our house.

> *It might sound strange, but I don't know now if these incidents of very odd family life, child neglect — whatever you could call it — bothered me more than the abuse. With the abuse, I knew it was going to happen, I knew what to expect and I just had to be very strong and it would be over until the next time. It's hard to explain this, but I believe that children who suffer long-term abuse must develop some sort of immunity, some way of dealing with it — which is what happened to me, otherwise I can't even consider what the outcome would have been.*

Being abandoned in an unfamiliar park or a strange pub was a very different matter. I never knew when it was going to happen again, or where it would be, or who would be there or what would happen... it's the 'not knowing' that is the worst thing, and always there was that biggest fear of not knowing if, this time, I would actually get back home, if I would ever see Mom again. By this time, I knew my relationship with Dad was fading, weakening. It was as if I was being pulled away from both my parents. The thoughts of what could happen if I really did get lost, too far from home, among strangers, were too awful to consider, and far more scary than Derek's vile treatment of me. Maybe this meant I was simply getting used to the abuse as it became more and more regular, more able to tolerate it... I really don't know. The abuse was getting to the stage where I couldn't even fetch a bucket of coal for the fire, to help Mom, without Derek attacking me. He would pin me against the wall in the coal shed and he'd have his fingers in me, or he would be forcing his penis into my hands, then into my mouth. I hated him more and more, and I was terrified of him, too. I thought, if nobody ever noticed what he was doing to me, would anyone notice if he actually killed me? And would that be more painful than the abuse? And – worse than all of this – would anyone care? When he was pushing himself into my mouth, I couldn't breathe, I felt I was choking and the taste made me want to be sick. Even when I was choking and gagging, Derek would just grab my hair and push my head down further until it felt like his penis was touching my tonsils, and I couldn't push away any more with my tongue.

When he had finished, he'd help me carry the coal back into the house, all the while repeating his threats to keep me quiet, making sure I knew what would happen if I ever dared tell on him. *"Dad will kill Mom, 'cos he'll blame her... He'll kill you for doing it... Nobody will believe you. You'll get took away."* He'd almost spit the words at me – anything he could think of to scare the life out of me.

When I look back at our home life, it was very strange, to say the least. Having a bath in the kitchen sink, where everyone could just walk in, a bathroom with no lock on the door, only carbolic soap to wash with, including my hair (unless I could sneak the Sunlight washing-up liquid in from the kitchen – but when I did manage to use this to wash myself, my hands would come out in cracked sores). If we ever caught 'nits', we'd have paraffin put in our hair and we'd be sat for what seemed like hours with it in, then soap would be scrubbed into our scalps to wash the paraffin out. We had torn strips of newspaper tied to a nail on the back of the toilet door that we had to use as toilet paper, and there was never a lock on the door, giving Derek yet another opportunity to be a pervert. The latch had a hole in it that he would peer through when I was on the toilet – I would try to block the hole with a screwed-up piece of newspaper but he would just push it through from the other side. Sometimes, he would actually get caught doing this but all that would happen was he'd be told off for 'teasing' me, and that would be the end of it. There really was no escape for me and it's amazing how alone you can feel in a house so full of people, where none of the others seem to know, or want to know, what's happening to you, right under their noses.

There were times when some of our relatives would come to visit with their kids, and we would all be sent to bed while they were still downstairs with Mom and Dad – we could hear the TV playing children's cartoons, like Woody Woodpecker and Road Runner, and it was still daylight outside! This was, of course, not something any of us could tolerate and, on one such occasion, we kept asking if we could go downstairs, calling to Dad and pleading with him. We went as far as to send little paper aeroplanes over the banister with messages written on them.

Then, as we weren't getting anywhere with this, I was sent downstairs with some begging notes to give to Dad – again, because I was 'daddy's little girl', the others believed he would listen to me and I would win him round. But Dad never listened to anybody, not even Mom.

This time, we thought this strategy had worked, when Dad shouted at Mom to fetch all the others downstairs, which she did. There we all stood, and suddenly Dad bellowed that he was going to put a stop to us pestering him with all our shouting and calling to him from upstairs when we were supposed to have been in bed. He ordered Mom to hold us between her legs with our arms pinned back, as he announced that he was going to burn our tongues out, so – of course – the others pushed me to the front to be the first to receive whatever punishment he was about to dole out. Mom did exactly as she was told because she was scared of him, too. He reached for the poker, which he'd left in the fire and which was now glowing orangey-red, as Mom held me firmly with my head locked in between her knees, and he spat out the command, *"Hold your tongue out!"*

I was terrified, but I was used to pain from Derek's abuse, and I thought if I couldn't use my tongue to tell Mom and Dad about what he was doing to me, then why did I need it? Tears were streaming down my face but I didn't speak, and then – as if in slow motion – I heard Dad shout for us all to go back up to bed, saying he didn't want to hear another word out of us again tonight. Once we were all under the covers, none of us spoke or moved again until morning. I often wonder, if I hadn't been first in line, would he have gone through with his dreadful threat? Or maybe his affection for me stopped him and saved us all that night?

> *That was just one example of how the older kids would use me as a 'risk assessment' to see if Dad would hurt me or let me go, and Mom would always play along with him, which makes me ask myself, did she hate me as much as my siblings did? How could she be a part of causing harm to one of her children? The answer to this is one word – FEAR. Like a lot of families in those times, mothers and children were ruled by fear, domestic violence was ignored and was swept under the carpet. No-one cared or chose to get involved. It was accepted as a part of normal life.*

And so, we only ventured downstairs when we knew Dad had gone out. This was clearly signalled by his habit of blowing his nose three times into his hanky just before he stepped out of the front door. We always had someone on watch at the front window so we knew when he was coming back, and we'd run upstairs as if the devil was after us, throw ourselves into bed and pretend to be asleep.

Whenever there was a thunderstorm, we'd all huddle together on the floor, wrapped in blankets to keep us safe in case a thunderbolt came through the house!

> *I later found out Mom was really scared of thunder and lightning, and so these huddling sessions were more for her benefit, rather than us being allowed any leeway.*

Derek was becoming more blatant with the sexual abuse, because it seemed he would never be found out. I believed, even if someone did discover what was going on, he'd still get away with everything. The way my life was going, I'd probably get the blame. So, my situation took a turn for the worse when he started taking me to his bedroom by sneaking me upstairs and locking his bedroom door behind us. It seemed he had padlocks on everything these days and he was taking control of the entire house. He would force me to strip off and get into his bed with him. This was much more of an invasion for me, because being naked means you are completely exposed, vulnerable – it was too intimate. Derek was a fat boy with thick ginger hair and he wasn't fussy about personal hygiene. He was still wetting the bed, despite having a big square margarine tub under his bed for him to pee in. The tub was always full to the brim because he was too lazy to empty it. His bed smelled so strongly of pee – it was a stench that made my eyes sting, and I had no idea how he could sleep like that.

> at smell sometimes starts to come over me, just as sickening as it was then, and I physically shudder when I see those large margarine tubs. These things never leave me, but at least today I can live with them.

There, in Derek's bed, suffocating in the disgusting smells and with his fat, sweaty body pressing against my little bony frame, he would push my head under the covers then start forcing his penis into my mouth. I had learnt to hold my tongue to the roof of my mouth as hard as I could, but nothing would stop Derek. I once started to sink my teeth into his penis, but all I got for my efforts was a punch to the back of my head and then he forced me down even further with both his hands until he was choking me again, and I'd hear his whispered threat, *"Do that again and I will kill you!"*

I battled in this way until my head and my body couldn't sink any further into the stinking piss-stained mattress, and then I'd have to give in. Then, at least, it would all be over quicker and I could get away from the smell and the repulsion.

When he had finished with me these days, he'd give me fifty pence to keep me quiet, along with the usual threats. I suppose, being a child, I didn't mind having the money – totally separate from how I got it – because our family didn't have very much and we certainly didn't get pocket money. At least now, I could fill my face with pop, crisps and sweets, and I didn't have to share with anyone – unless they caught me with my treats, in which case they'd take them off me. I could never tell Mom they'd stolen my goodies because she'd want to know where I got the money from to pay for them.

> *I was being paid for sex, no matter how you look at the situation. For many years into my adult life, I couldn't come to terms with this, and consequently, I would never accept gifts from anyone, even Eric.*

When I saw the grocery van pull up outside one day, without thinking, I ran out with Mom to buy myself some sweets. Immediately, she asked where I'd got the money from and I said I'd found it in the back garden. Mom was furious because she said she'd dropped her purse while pegging the washing out and all her change had fallen out – so she took it off me! All that pain, for nothing. It wasn't fair but I could hardly tell her, *"Oh, no, it's mine. It's what Derek pays me for sexually abusing me and me keeping quiet"*.

When the Crocodile Smile Club came to Harden Junior school, they gave out free tubes of toothpaste and my friend, Helen, squirted a whole tube down my throat. I wasn't feeling at all well after this, and I just wanted to sleep in a chair in the living room. I had started trying to protect myself from Derek's attacks, and I'd wrapped myself in a blanket and curled up in a tight ball with the edges of the blanket tucked under my feet and my arms, thinking this would give me enough 'armour' to catch a few minutes' sleep. I woke up to find Derek with his tongue between my legs: there was no escape, no peace. I kicked him away and ran out to where Mom was chatting to neighbours at the front gate. Maybe it was because I felt ill, maybe because I was tired, or maybe I just couldn't take any more – whatever it was, I was starting to fight back.

By this time, I wasn't getting much rest, being too scared to go to sleep in case Derek came to pluck me out of the bed in the middle of the night. I would wrap myself in the crochet blankets Mom made, by poking my toes through the holes to anchor the cover at one end, and I'd do the same with my fingers, then I'd wedge myself between Brenda and Shaun. But even this didn't work… nothing worked, and Derek would always get me.

School holidays came round, and Mom would have me, Nigel and Craig under her feet, as she put it, so Derek would offer to take us conker picking in Linley Woods in Rushall. As soon as we got there, he'd send the two boys off to collect conkers, telling them not to come back until he fetched them, and then he'd pin me down to the ground among the damp leaves and twigs, and his hands would be in my pants, prodding and fumbling about. In broad daylight, in a public place – and no-one seeing, no-one noticing anything, no-one caring?

Another time when we little ones were under Mom's feet, Derek offered to take us all upstairs to bed and get us to sleep. There was no such thing as TV sets in bedrooms back then, so going to bed meant going to sleep right away. Derek put Nigel and Craig in the bed, tight up against the wall, he got in the middle and I was on the edge. He threatened the boys to get to sleep and he was already fumbling in my pants as he was talking to them. They were soon fast asleep, and that's when Derek tried to penetrate me but, of course, I screamed out in pain and started crying. Craig woke up at the noise and asked why I was crying. Derek told him he'd slapped my legs because I was fidgeting about, and he told Craig to roll over and go back to sleep. But both Nigel and Craig were restless now and were soon wide awake, so Derek took them downstairs to Mom, having first told me to pretend to be asleep. He padlocked the door, leaving me locked in the room on my own. I was terrified, because I knew he wasn't finished with me, so I tried very hard to go to sleep, but he was soon back at the door, unlocking it and then locking us in together.

He made me take all my clothes off and he did the same. I wanted to be sick, to run away, to escape, but, as always, I froze and he got on top of the bedclothes, pushing me down. Then he had his tongue inside me, his fingers inside me, then he started forcing his penis into me. I felt like I was being burnt by flames and being torn apart at the same time. I was crying, pleading with him to stop hurting me. Instead of stopping, he put his hand over my mouth to stifle the noise of my cries, my screaming. His hand was covering my nose as well, so I couldn't breathe, and his fat, smelly weight was crushing me as he pushed and pushed until I was raw, crying, my tears soaking me. It seemed like such a long time, because I hadn't been able to block it out this time. This time the pain had taken over my body and my head, and I couldn't escape outside myself like I'd learned to do before. The pain was evil, and was still the same, even when he got out of me. I remembered Dad heating the poker until it was red hot and I felt like I'd been abused with that poker. Even in my sorry state, obviously in great pain, crying and sobbing, Derek wouldn't let me out of the room until I promised to shut up crying and not say anything.

Mom was downstairs, cooking tea, so I limped straight to the bathroom and ran a cold bath. We could only have hot baths on a Sunday, ready for school the next day. Hot water, any other time, was only for Dad. I put a basket of dirty washing against the door so no-one could get in, while I sat in the cold water, trying to soothe my private parts down. The water never felt so good, and I'd never before been so grateful for having a cold bath, as I picked up the block of carbolic soap and started scrubbing myself. I was stinging now, down below, unsure if that was from the horrible soap or if it was still the pain from earlier.

Just then, Dad barged in to get a shave before he went out for the evening, pushing the wash basket out of the way. If I'd stood up then, with only a hand towel to cover myself, Dad would have said, *"I've seen it all before, Bones"*, so I had to sit in the cold, murky, scummy water, with my knees pulled up under my chin, until he finished his shave. I still felt dirty, because now I was starting to realise I was no longer a child who was unashamed of her body, but a child who had been stripped of her last bit of innocence, a child confused as to what had just happened, and unable to work out why any of it was being allowed to happen.

When I went into friends' houses in the street I would sit still, not daring to speak, waiting to see if they treated their children the way I was being treated – if I could see that, it might make some sense. My friend Penny's dad used to march around the house, from room to room, preaching the Bible, walking round with the good book open as he read from it and shouting the words to anyone who was listening. I see this as brainwashing people with fear, which is just another form of what I was going through back then.

In my friend Helen's house, things were very different, but just as dysfunctional. Her mother was very quiet, and her grandmother would visit, all dressed up like royalty (compared to anyone I'd ever seen) in smart blouses and suits, with her hair neat and tidy, immaculate make-up and wearing a pearl necklace with matching ear-rings. Helen's dad was always coming home drunk, starting an argument with her mom and then hitting her – while we kids were sitting there. When this happened, we'd run to my house and tell my mom, and she'd get Derek to go up to Helen's house and throw her dad out. Helen thought Derek was wonderful because he was big and strong and could sort her dad out. Nobody else could see that he was just a bully.

Our family was beginning to get a bad reputation now. We were people to avoid, to be afraid of, there were so many of us and we were known for all the wrong reasons – for stealing, for fighting…

One evening, Sean Wayne was beaten up by a

family with a similar reputation, because their dad had made advances to our mom while she was out shopping and she'd made it clear she wasn't interested. Dad had found out and he got Derek to beat up one of the family's boys and so they got Sean Wayne back for that. They all turned up at our house in their car and all our boys were standing together at the front gate, all armed with swords from Dad's collection. Derek stood at the very front and the car stopped. He picked the front end of the car up and turned it over. As one of them got out of the car to run away, Dad swung at him with the sword.

The fear and worry of what might happen after this episode was overwhelming. Would that family come back again, would someone be killed, would Dad have a heart attack, or would he have to go to prison...? If Dad went away, Derek would be far worse, if that was possible. It was particularly frightening for me to see just how strong he was, and suddenly, his threats meant more than before. If he could turn a car over, he could kill me with no problem. I wasn't as strong as a toy car, let alone a real, full-size one.

Probably because I wasn't able to say or do anything at home about Derek and the abuse, I started 'pushing my luck' at school, by giving the teachers my evil looks, 'sly eyes', which was my way of making a statement against everyone in my life telling me what to do all the time, everyone controlling me. Given the ever-worsening abuse, this was hardly a big reaction, and the teachers wouldn't tell me off, but they would mention it in my reports and they'd tell Mom at parents' evenings how rude I was when asked to do anything, I never refused to do what they told me, I would just give them my best attempt at a really black look. If they'd had even the slightest inkling of what was churning around inside my young head, they would have realised they were getting off very lightly indeed. It was my way of doing something to fight back against all the control, rather than continue to do nothing. It was my release, my safety valve.

In spite of everything that was happening, I was doing really well in some areas of my education. I was very good at maths and was top of the class, together with my friend, Terrence. I sang in the school choir and played the trombone, even winning a place in the Walsall Orchestra while I was at junior school. The orchestra met at Bluecoat school in Walsall for practice sessions and, once again, I was at the mercy of my siblings to take me there. As expected, after Diane taking me a few times, she stopped, so I couldn't get there and I eventually lost my place in the orchestra. What I really lost was the escape I experienced through the music.

I was even in the school gymnastics club and I excelled at those events I favoured. The school put me forward to race against schools in other boroughs for a championship award, and, on the day I was competing, I accidentally tripped another female runner on the track, so I stopped to help her get up and to apologise. My form teacher, Mr Golightly, wasn't a happy bunny. He was shouting and calling me names ('stupid' was among them), but I didn't care – it didn't involve physical pain, so I could block him out. The skill of being able to do this has been my saving grace and has enabled me to survive.

Derek was beginning to realise his strength and power, and so he was becoming more daring in his efforts to abuse me at every opportunity. He was definitely becoming more cruel. Added to this, I wasn't managing my fear as well as I had been doing before, and I tried to come up with ways of protecting myself from his attacks. I started wearing two pairs of pants – one pair under my woolly tights and one over the top of them. I was trying to wrap myself away, out of reach.

One day when Derek had caught me and forced me into the bed, and I simply couldn't fight him, after just having penetrated me vaginally, he turned me over and penetrated me anally with such force I felt my insides were falling out, and the pain was so great I almost passed out. This time, he was using some petroleum jelly that Craig had been using for his 'cherry lips' – a red sore that had formed around his mouth because he kept licking his lips. I knew at that moment that I couldn't take any more of this. I wanted to die. That night, in my bed, I prayed I would catch some illness and die, or

Derek would really, actually kill me. I never wished so hard for anything, over and over again. I was beaten.

Derek would try to catch me on the stairs after this, but I would tell him, *"NO!"* and I'd threaten to tell Mom. As always, his reply was, *"Dad will kill you, and Mom as well!"*

> In later life, I found out that Mom had been abused by her own father, had become pregnant as a result and was forced into giving birth, but the baby had died. This made sense of a lot of the past, in the way Dad treated Mom, the way he casually had affairs, and the way Derek ruled Mom through fear.

So, now there was no way I could ever win. I was trying to fight but was far too afraid, so I tried keeping out of the way by staying away from the house and spending time at friends' homes as much as possible.

Then, one day, Mom called me into the kitchen and there was another woman there with her, someone with long, dark hair. They were sat on two chairs, side by side, and Mom asked me to get on her lap and lie across both of them, which I did. Mom then put some cream on my 'tuppence' down below, as we called it, and she asked me outright if Derek had been doing anything to me.

Oh, what a relief! I started crying and told her

he had been 'shagging' me, which is how he referred to the abuse. Then I ran upstairs, just crying and crying. In the bedroom, I was met by Diane and her friend, a dark-haired girl whose mom owned a local shop. Diane wanted to know why I was crying, what had happened, and I blurted out, *"Derek's been shagging me!"* Diane's friend left at this point and never came back. Although I knew what Derek was doing was wrong, I didn't really understand the meaning of the word 'shagging' and I had no idea what a strong word it was.

This event opened a door to yet another unforeseen nightmare, as Diane saw her opportunity. She began blackmailing me, constantly threatening to tell Dad if I didn't do as she wanted me to. Because Derek had made me believe that Dad would really kill me if he found out, I was terrified now that Diane would tell. I knew Diane had her own hold over Mom because Mom used to confide in her… I was so confused and didn't know who or what to believe now, which is why, today, I will only deal with people who tell the truth, even if I don't like what I hear.

I loved being a tomboy, and this proved to be very useful. Once, when Pat came to visit Craig, she brought me, Nigel and Craig a net bag of marbles each, and Derek chased us all down the hallway, trying to snatch mine out of my hand – but he tripped and fell over. I picked up the bag of marbles, swung it round in the air and hit Derek in the head with it, as hard as I could. This cut a big gash in his eyebrow, there was blood everywhere and he was sitting on the floor, crying and screaming, *"I can't see! I can't see!"* but this was just the blood running down into his eye.

All those years of abuse, all the anger, the frustration, the disgust, the pain, the hatred ... it all exploded right there, right then. That's when I realised I could hurt him, just as he had hurt me – but I had the choice. I didn't *want* to hurt him, I just wanted him to leave me alone.

Chapter three

Blaming myself

To prove that everything in life is relative, now I was living with Pat and Steve most of the time, I was happier and more content than I'd ever been because I had escaped the madness of life at Mom and Dad's, I was well away from the taunting and tormenting from the other kids, and I could sleep at night because I was sharing a room with my lovely niece, Hayley, who was more like a younger sister to me and who I had loved and adored from the minute she was born. We were just two little girls, tucked up together, without a care in the world. Most of all, I was safely out of reach of Derek, after the years of abuse and cruelty.

The 'relative' aspect of this is that I was now treated as some sort of servant in my new home, but I didn't mind, didn't care. I would have gladly accepted far worse treatment if it meant being able to live well away from Derek's grasp. It was as if my prayers – those desperate thoughts I'd had in the worst and darkest moments of my life – had finally been answered.

As with everything, there was a bit of a downside because Pat and Steve, quite rightly, liked to have their house to themselves at weekends and so I'd have to return to Mom and Dad's, taking Craig and Hayley with me. I do know that Pat would ask Dad for money for having me there through the week, but he would tell her, *"You wanted her, you pay for her!"* – as if I was some possession being passed around, or a pet dog! It did make me wonder, though, because one of the things my siblings had always taunted me about was that I was adopted. I did begin to wonder if this could be true.

My new happiness was to prove short-lived when Steve decided to re-decorate Hayley's bedroom, which meant Hayley and I were moved in to the bigger room. Craig shared this room with my sister Diane's boyfriend, David, who had started lodging at Pat and Steve's. They shared a bed by the window and our bed was just inside the door by the airing cupboard. One night, Diane and David had come back to the house and Diane decided she would stay the night, so the sleeping arrangements were changed. David and Craig would have their bed, as normal, Diane and I would share the other bed in the same room, and Hayley would get in with Pat and Steve. I was already asleep, tucked right up against the wall, and

Craig was asleep in his bed, when Diane and David came in. Diane got into bed beside me, which woke me up but I didn't let on I was awake. David was asking her for sex and she was refusing him; the next thing, my whole body was jolted as David punched Diane hard in her back as she lay next to me.

In an instant, all of my old fears rushed through my mind, and I started thinking I would be next – I was terrified, back in that stinking, piss-stained bed in Keats Road, and my body was trembling, shivering as if I was freezing cold. Diane tried to comfort me but she was crying herself.

> *I often thought, after that horrible episode, if I felt everything that was happening to Diane because I was next to her in the bed, why didn't anyone ever see or hear or suspect what Derek was doing to me for all of that time – and then I realised, even though I knew what was happening to Diane, I had been frozen with fear and I hadn't done or said anything, so maybe it was the same for everybody.*

The bedroom decorating was almost finished, with the new red spotty wallpaper, when David came into the bedroom one night after we'd all fallen asleep

Hayley and me in our bed, and Craig over by the window in his. I woke with a start to find David leaning over me, rummaging under the bedclothes, his hands tugging at my knickers. Since the abuse, I had started wearing knickers to bed, as I felt it gave me some protection – however slight. I was wide awake but pretended to be asleep, hoping he would go away and leave me alone. But he didn't. He pushed his fingers inside me then he took hold of my hands and started pushing them towards his penis. I had to do something. I let him know I was awake now, and I told him to leave me alone or else I'd tell Diane. David stopped. Then he apologised, saying he was sorry, that he and Diane had just argued. This was very strange to me – getting an apology – and I believed him, believed this was just a silly mistake on his part and that it wouldn't happen again. I was reassured the next morning when David apologised to me again, and asked me not to tell Pat and Steve. So I didn't. I believed him. After all, he had apologised and Derek never did that, so this must be different. It was a normal Thursday night and the bedroom decorating was still not finished, because Steve worked full-time in a foundry and was finding it difficult to give the decorating the time and energy it needed. Hayley and I were tucked up in the bed by the airing cupboard and Craig was in his bed by the window. They were both asleep but I was still awake because I had to wait until the whole house was settled before I would relax enough to be able to sleep.

David came into the room and, instead of putting himself to bed with Craig, he got into our bed beside me. Straight away, he was fumbling around with his fingers in me, then, without a word and before I had a chance to think what to do, he was on top of me and I was being raped. All I could think of was Hayley, sleeping beside me. I was scared she would wake up and see what was happening to me, and then she'd have to live with that image for the rest of her life. I knew, only too well, what that was like and I couldn't ever inflict the same awful thing on her. I was scared, too, in case David was going to do anything to her as well, in case he hurt her. It wasn't the first time someone had forced themselves on me – I was already abused, damaged, harmed... I'd already had my childhood taken from me, and, because of all the abuse that had gone before, I could sort of deal with it in my own way, but Hayley was younger and beautifully innocent. I couldn't let this happen to her, whatever it took. I loved her and I just wanted to protect her.

David got off me and – to my amazement – he apologised again, just like the other time, excusing his filthy behaviour by blaming the drink he'd had, blaming yet another argument with Diane. I couldn't believe my ears, but what came next was so far beyond belief, I couldn't take it in for a few moments. He said, *"Diane told me about you and Derek, and she said nobody would believe you if it happened again."*

I felt someone had hit me in the head with a hammer; I couldn't believe what I had just heard. I was hurled, in an instant, into yet another nightmare as I realised, not only had my sister's boyfriend raped me, but it was my sister – my flesh and blood – who had given him the idea and set him up to do it.

I was numb. One of my own siblings had abused me for years, had harmed me, hurt me, with never a single thought for my feelings, my physical pain, my state of mind… and now, another of my 'family', not happy that she'd used that abuse to blackmail me and bully me and control me, had actively encouraged her own boyfriend to rape me. As if that wasn't bad enough, she had also put Hayley at risk – knowing I would put my own life on the line to protect her.

> *I knew, at the moment this brutal reality hit me, that I would never forgive Diane, however long I lived or whatever happened to either of us. I never have.*

Keeping such dark secrets had become part of my everyday life, and I carried on as normal after this, going to school, collecting Hayley and Craig from neighbours at the end of the day and catching the bus to Corporation Street in Caldmore, to Mom and Dad's for the weekend, as usual.

I had learned to 'brush myself off, pick myself up and start all over again'. Or so I thought, until later in my life when the realisation hit me that I had just been putting everything in boxes and storing them all away at the back of my mind, to protect myself. Over the weekend, I didn't say anything to Mom because David's words rang in my ears, *"Nobody will believe you"*. After all, for this to happen, with not just one person doing these things to me, but two, and without any witnesses, without anyone having a clue that it was going on, in houses where there were so many other people at the time… everyone would say it was impossible. There would be questions: why didn't I stop him? Why didn't I scream? Why didn't I tell anyone? Why? Why? Why? If I had no answers to these questions myself, how did I expect I'd cope if the others asked me the same things, which I knew they would? I started to think it must all be my fault, somehow. Both Derek and then David had got into my head and they would stay there for a long time, until one day when I would come to understand it all myself. I had to hope for that day to come.

> *Looking back, I was more able to come to terms with the abuse because, all through that time, I was a child, whereas the rape happened to me when I was becoming more of an adult physically, even though my mind was still that of a child. This was probably made somewhat easier because, all my life, I'd been controlled by others in every aspect — choosing my friends, where I went, what I did, choosing a boyfriend, keeping me close within the family group, not allowing me to try things for myself in case I became*

independent of them and would finally be able to stand up and ask the questions I needed the answers to.

As the weekend drew to a close, and it would soon be time to go back to Pat and Steve's, I knew I couldn't go. I was between the devil and the deep blue sea, but the better option, for now, was definitely Mom and Dad's house. I could go back to my 'better life' once Hayley's room was finished. In the meantime, I could still take Craig and Hayley to school, as long as I caught the earlier bus… my frantic reasoning wasn't really working for me, especially as Pat and Steve were trying their hardest to get me to go back with them, then Dad suddenly stepped in, saying bluntly, *"She can stay at home for good"*. It wasn't much of a choice – staying in the house where Derek was, or sleeping in the room where David was. I would take my chances at home and sleep in Mom's bed, until I could see a way out of the situation.

Mom said I could walk into Walsall on Monday with Derek, as he would be going in to work at the same time as I needed to get to school. I knew there was no way I would be on my own with him and I started planning how I would lag behind: I could think of a few things I could use to delay leaving the house long enough for Derek to be well on his way before I set off. Derek was now really huge, like a giant, whereas David was quite slim build, so I knew, if I couldn't stop David, I would have absolutely no chance with Derek.

My plan was working, as Derek was halfway down Midland Road, so I set off. It was snowing now, and I hadn't walked far when David's car pulled up alongside me. Diane was in the passenger seat and she was telling me to get in the car, saying Dad had said I had to go with them and they would drop me off at school... Something snapped. I was suddenly outside myself, watching *me* standing there, shouting at them, cursing and swearing, threatening to tell Dad about them... My language was terrible but I wasn't in control for that few moments. David drove off quickly, telling Diane to leave me be. I don't know who was more scared – me or them.

Left standing there on my own, I was suddenly back in my own head. I noticed a crowd had gathered outside the Co-op Dairy yard, and these men had been watching the 'goings-on'. They were shouting things like, *"Go on, girl, you tell 'em!"* and I was so embarrassed because my language had been so awful, but I was also mad at myself because I had allowed myself to be pushed to this level. The one thing I had fought so hard for, was NOT to be like them, the family. I never wanted to have a big mouth like Pat, never wanted to be a prostitute like Brenda, never wanted to be evil like Diane, never wanted to fall into drinking, drugs, lying, cheating, stealing... like the rest of them. My role models, God help me. I hated to think I could ever turn out like any of them.

Back at Pat and Steve's, the bedroom was eventually finished. Not long after this, Diane and David got a flat together in Dolphin Close, just down the road from Pat's, so I could now go back without worrying about David. The only thing was, Dad wouldn't have any of this and told me I couldn't go. I was running upstairs, crying my eyes out, when Mom followed me into the bedroom. I told her I wanted my birth certificate, that I didn't belong to this family, that I wanted to go back to Pat and Steve's, I hated Derek, I would kill myself... Mom must have realised I was at the end of my tether. She said she would answer to Dad and that I should go to Pat and Steve's and stay there for good. And that's what I did. I would be safe, now David had gone.

Some weeks later David and Diane had been arguing and he had dropped her off by the local chippy. She appeared at Pat and Steve's, all messed up and with her clothes ripped off her back, saying David had raped her. Pat and Steve called the police and I went upstairs with the kids while they interviewed Diane. Not long after this, both Diane and David were taken in to Walsall Manor hospital after they had both taken an overdose. Diane saw a psychiatrist who wanted her to be admitted, but Mom and Dad wouldn't allow this – no doubt they were worried about what she might tell the doctors. Another classic case of sweeping things under the carpet, rather than confronting them.

The subject of mental health still carried a certain stigma at that time, and most definitely within the working classes, but Diane needed professional help and she was being denied it. The others teased her, saying she had sent the psychiatrist mad – I hated them for this, even though she had been so cruel to me in the past.

> *I knew then that 'the family' were never going to help me, and that I was the only one who could change my life. This is what I decided to do, and my plan was to work hard at school and do well so I could have a better future – and to move well away from the past.*

Chapter four

Making my own decisions

When I was in the fifth year at school and it was time to choose my options, I decided I would like to take Law as I was interested in becoming a solicitor, or even a barrister. A big influence on this choice was that my teacher at Forest Comprehensive, Mr Dowd, was very different from the other teachers because he treated the students like equals, and he spoke to us as adults. He was from Liverpool, and he had a beard and long hair – a bit like John Lennon! He told me that my brother, Shaun, had once given him the fright of his life by jumping out from behind the cupboards that divided the classrooms. Although this had really scared Mr Dowd, instead of saying Shaun was an idiot or anything like that, he found it quite funny and he called Shaun 'a character'. I liked Mr Dowd.

In the sixth form, I carried on studying Law, still with Mr Dowd as my tutor, and I loved everything about the subject – civil law, criminal law, the visits to

Walsall Magistrates' Court and to Birmingham Crown Court. I thought it was amazing to actually be able to observe cases being presented, being argued, and being lost or won. Whenever I heard the court's decision on a case, I would think to myself that I was probably the only one in my family who had ever been in front of a judge without it being the result of getting into trouble with the law!

During my Law course, Dad got me an interview at Geoffens Solicitors in Townsend Square, for a job that would give me the chance to start at the bottom and work my way up. That appealed to me, but, even if I didn't get the job, just having the interview at a law firm would be great experience. My very first interview! So, whatever the outcome, I saw the situation as a win-win. The day of the interview came and I was very nervous, seeing that I had absolutely no idea what to expect.

I entered the building and was met at Reception by an older lady who didn't make me feel any less uncomfortable – she didn't smile once, and she just gave me sort of commands, *"Come through. Sit down."* I wasn't even offered anything to drink, but I was kept waiting for what seemed like hours and no-one bothered to apologise for the delay. It all added to my feelings of unease and apprehension, and my nervous state. Then I was called to go through to Mr Geoffens' office. I had to walk through an office that was full of men – not one female in sight. They all looked at me, some of them really stared, and I felt very young and awkward.

I remember thinking that I couldn't possibly do this every day. Because of the things that had happened to me in the past, situations like this – however ordinary they might be to other people – could easily throw me into a panic attack or bring on severe nausea. Simple things that other (normal?) people wouldn't even register would make me feel very uneasy and I'd have an awful urge to run away. I knew then that I needed to get control, otherwise, if I let *it* rule *me*, I'd never be able to function in ordinary everyday circumstances – in fact, my life would be over. I just couldn't accept that. I had survived long-term abuse and I had survived rape (not to mention the mental and emotional abuse that went on within the family), and now it was a choice – either I take over and win this battle, or *it* would take over *me*, my whole life.

There, in that solicitor's office, I made my decision that I was choosing to take my life back, take it into my control. I wasn't going to be afraid again if some man stood next to me or looked at me, or spoke to me, interacted with me in any way... I would have my own boundaries for my own protection, but without this interfering with my life.

Over the years that followed, I think I must have done quite a good job of reprogramming my thinking in this way, because, among the lovely friends I have, there are quite a few men and I feel very comfortable around them.

There I was, sat in Mr Geoffens' office, having what I believed was an interview, but it was more him talking about the friendship he had with my dad and the good times they'd had together. He told me the job was mine, starting as a trainee legal secretary and with the prospect of carrying on with my studies to further my knowledge of law. When I went home and told Dad the good news that I'd got the job, he already knew. Apparently, the 'interview' was just a formality... this set me thinking now – did I get this job because of me and how I presented myself, how I came across, or because of my dad? If it was Dad's doing, what would he want of me...? My main thought was that he probably saw this as a way to use me to 'keep him legal' when he was up to no good, stealing and the like (which was very often). Did he think, once I'd learned the job, I'd be able to sort things out for him whenever he needed me to? If so, this would mean I would still be in Dad's control, still doing what he told me to do. I couldn't accept this, and I wasn't going to play ball. I wasn't going to have anyone telling me what to do any more, especially family, because that would mean something bad would happen if they were involved. I wouldn't do it, I'd had enough of obeying orders.

And so, that day, I walked away from a job I

would have loved, working in law, just as I'd studied for and hoped for. But I don't regret it for one minute. Earning money isn't all it's made out to be – happiness is the most important thing.

What happened that day, and how I dealt with it, based on the decisions I made *for myself*, taught me a lot and also put me in good stead to take control of my future. I've never taken a job just for the wages: when I worked for the bookies, I even turned down having a contract so that I could have more flexibility with my hours, and the silly thing is, I never took advantage of this because I loved the job and the customers so much, I wanted to be there all the time! And if someone asks me for my help, I'll do everything in my power to help them, but if they try to *tell me* to do something, I'll dig my heels in firmly.

I learned a lot that day. I learned that I had choices, I learned that I was no longer a child, and I learned that family aren't always right just because they are family, and they don't necessarily know what's best for you. Most importantly, I learned to take control of my own life and my own destination.

Chapter five

Leaving school

Carrying on the newly acquired independence, I made my first step into the world of employment by taking a job at a holiday camp, along with my friend, Jane. We had thought we would be able to work together and share lodgings, which would have been good, but we were placed in two different holiday camps – she went to St Ives and I went to Seaton in Devon.

A group of us newly recruited 'children's entertainers' attended staff training in Skegness before taking up our posts and one of my colleagues soon acquired the nickname 'Seagull' because he would get drunk and then run around the camp site squealing like a seagull!

The holiday camp was OK, with caravans, chalets and a clubhouse. I was sharing the accommodation with one other girl and our lodgings left a lot to be desired – my bed was on bricks! Rent was deducted from our wages and we had to buy our own food. Seagull and I worked together, starting each day early with children's games and activities, a children's club and so on, then snatching a quick break before the evening entertainment began. This was the fun time of the day, with party dances – my favourite was the 'Time Warp' from the Rocky Horror show – and the evening would end with all the staff getting together for the finale. It was hard work and long hours, but I really enjoyed looking after the children: seeing them having such fun running around together, their laughter and their smiling faces gave me a lot of pleasure and I loved helping them to enjoy just being children – something I'd missed out on.

The staff would arrange to get together in each other's chalets, even though this wasn't allowed. Our chalet was the farthest from the clubhouse and so it was the obvious choice for such events, as there would be less chance of being found out. One evening, Seagull had asked me if I would go for a walk with him and, because we were colleagues, I thought that would be OK. As soon as we started to walk, he put his arm around my shoulders – as if we were a couple! Then he asked if we could go for a drink, at which point I froze and felt sick. I suggested we go to the clubhouse, as I thought it would be safer there. When we got there, Seagull told me he had no money and asked me to get the drinks; I did so, but I didn't want to be used for free drinks, so I made an excuse and went back to the chalet.

Having made a pact with my room-mate that we would not be bringing anyone back to the chalet, that same night she brought a group of men back, Seagull being one of them. I immediately felt scared because of how he'd been with me earlier. I was back to being that frightened little girl, too scared to go to sleep in case someone came into my room. My room mate was obviously very different from me and she entertained the men all night, laughing, joking around and having sex with them. I wanted to cover my ears to block it all out but I was more afraid of not hearing, in case someone came to get me. I was paralysed. All of those feelings from the past came flooding back until it felt like I would drown in them.

It wasn't long before my eldest sister, Pat, was ringing me at the holiday camp to say Dad was ill, and she put my niece, Hayley, on the phone, in tears and pleading with me to come home because she missed me. I caved in and went back to my former life of being the live-in nanny and housemaid to Pat and Steve, cooking, cleaning and looking after their two kids, Craig and Hayley. Often, Steve would go to collect Pat from her work at the bookmaker's and he'd tell me to get something for me and the kids to eat, saying he and Pat would get their own supper. Most of the time, I'd make beans on toast for us, then I'd get the kids to bed and I wouldn't see Pat and Steve again until well after midnight.

There was, however, a plus side to this

arrangement. At least I wasn't running around, getting endless cups of tea for everyone visiting at home, and beans on toast was far better than going back to the abuse, or the fear of it.

I did stay at Mom's at weekends and I struggled with this because Derek was still living there. The house was a three-storey Victorian building with an attic and a cellar – rooms to be avoided at all costs. Although the abuse had stopped at this point, nothing could stop me worrying and so I slept with Mom, Hayley and Craig, all together in a double bed – cramped, crushed and with very little chance of any sleep, but, at least, safe.

Chapter six

Finding my other half

The very first time I ever saw Eric was when my sister, Pat, was getting married – to Eric's half- brother, Stephen. Eric was sixteen and was Steve's best man, while I was all of ten years old and was Pat's bridesmaid.

I was a real tomboy, and Craig and I would mess about together on the school playing fields, climbing trees, swinging on the football posts, and burying each other in the sand pit. Craig was Pat's son from her first marriage and she had dumped him on my mom and dad when he was a baby. He lived with them right up until he was seven or eight. Then, one day, Pat just turned up and took him back with her. Once, I remember we were messing about in a tree when Eric came over and shouted at us to get down. I told Craig to ignore him, saying *"He's only your uncle"*, then Eric told me off and threatened to smack my arse. I shut up and clambered down, but I gave him the blackest look I could muster; I was angry at him for shouting at me – I could take physical pain but I absolutely hated people hurting my feelings.

Any time when I visited Steve and Eric's mom's house, I would bump into Eric and he would inevitably tease me for being cheeky. I'd sit in the living room with Craig and Eric's dad while Vera, Eric's mom, would try to feed me cakes, crisps and pop. I always said no to these offerings because I would never eat in front of anyone.

Vera could be found sitting in the kitchen, next to the sideboard with the plastic sliding doors and a drop-down worktop where you could cut bread or cake. This was the one thing I hated about visiting Eric's folks, because this cupboard was the same as the one that stood in the back garden at home and Derek used to lift me up on to it... just seeing it sent shivers through my bones.

Later, when I was growing up and starting secondary school, I would spend most of my time at Pat and Steve's, looking after Craig. After my stint at the holiday camp, I was living with them all the time, taking the kids to school on my way to work, and taking Craig and Hayley to my mom and dad's for weekends.

By now, Eric featured regularly in my life with his frequent visits, and I would wait on him hand and foot along with any other visitors. It was soon common knowledge that he'd left his wife.

Nobody could blame Eric for this break-up. He'd met this girl, Tracey, when he was working as a bouncer at Max' nightclub. He was living at home with his very controlling mother, Vera, a nasty woman who nagged him constantly and made his life a misery. Eric was unhappy and desperate to get away from home, and he threw himself into this new relationship – even though everyone warned him that she had a bad reputation.

Tracey would visit Eric's mom, and Vera very soon grew suspicious about all the hospital appointments Tracey was having, so she confronted the girl, asking her outright if she was pregnant. Tracey was feisty and didn't hold back: she told Vera the baby wasn't Eric's but that she planned to keep it. Vera asked her to have an abortion, as she could see Eric was being trapped, but Tracey stood her ground and eventually the baby was born. Vera never forgave her.

Eric moved in with Tracey's family until they found a flat of their own. He, being the good person he is, took the baby on as his own, hoping things would work out for them as a family. When they married, no-one from Eric's side went to the wedding, only Tracey's folks. As time went by, Tracey gave birth to Eric's child but things didn't go well at all. He started appearing at Pat and Steve's a lot more because she was always going out clubbing – drinking, dancing and spending time with other men. She resented having to 'settle down' at such a young age (she was seventeen when she and Eric got together) and was trying to re-live the youth she felt she'd lost.

Eric would escape the inevitable rows by walking along the canal bank to visit his dad – also named Eric, and a lovely, kindly man – then pop in on Pat and Steve. He said he was lonely. Sometimes he'd get home from work to find Tracey with her mates in the flat, all drinking cheap cider… she would go out to the shop, saying they needed some milk, but she'd have her clubbing outfit on and she wouldn't come back… he even turned the other cheek when men off the estate took pleasure in telling him they'd slept with his wife… but the final straw came when he had a phone call at work telling him they were being evicted because the rent hadn't been paid. Tracey was in the pub with the baby in the pram outside.

One evening when he came to Pat and Steve's, I was just about to go out with a 'boyfriend' who Pat had matched me with because she felt sorry for him and she said that, as I was now nineteen, I should have a boyfriend. I was only going along with this to keep the peace, but I didn't like the boy and, when Eric turned up, I offered to take him with us to meet some friends. An old school pal of mine, Jayne, took a shine to Eric and they arranged to meet the following week. I went with him to the King's Arms in Bloxwich to meet his date – but she never turned up.

The pub was always busy in those days, with

special Fun Nights when you could only get in if you had a ticket. It had a friendly atmosphere because a lot of the regular crowd lived nearby, so most of them knew each other. Eric and I sat talking all evening and then went on to a wine bar with some other friends. It was now winter, and was freezing cold in the evenings – not that the weather could stop us young girls wearing our little short skirts and high heels with no coat or jacket to protect us! Eric bought me my first ever martini and lemonade, which I hated, so he ended up drinking it. We sat all night beside a blow heater, talking and laughing, then Eric drove me and my friend home. As I was getting out of the car, he asked me if I would go out with him, so the next day I finished with the other boy, because, if I was going to start seeing Eric, that was the right thing to do.

It was November, 1987. Eric and I became a couple and he was the first boyfriend I'd had who was of my own choosing. To this day, we joke about how we only got together because my friend stood him up! I told Eric everything about my childhood, no holds barred. I wanted him to know me openly and honestly; I knew in him I had someone who cared for me, understood me, wanted to protect me – and who listened to me. From that time forward, I vowed always to talk about things and never to keep secrets.

Chapter seven

Getting away from it all

Eric had been living with his mom in her rented council bungalow since he and Tracey had split up, and he was having a really bad time, missing his children like mad, going through a really nasty separation and with no home of his own. Then Vera told him he'd have to move out and find somewhere else, because she was worried about getting into trouble for having a lodger. And so, Eric came to live with me at Pat and Steve's.

When we'd been together getting on for a year, we noticed an advert in the paper for jobs abroad, so we contacted the people and went for an interview, but it turned out to be selling timeshares so we weren't interested.

We mentioned to Pat about this, and she was really annoyed and wouldn't speak to me. She said we should have told her beforehand! Eric was working at the bakery and his shifts were all staggered hours. Whenever he was at home, Pat would sit and chat with both of us but, as soon as he went off to work, she wouldn't say another word to me. She still expected me to be her 'servant', doing the cooking, cleaning, looking after Hayley and Craig... I even had to get up early in the mornings to do her hair for her! I would also make it my job to get the children out of the way when she and Steve were fighting – there would be chairs being flung around, ornaments flying across the room, even knives being thrown.

I'd scoop Hayley up in my arms and get her and Craig upstairs, out of harm's way, as quickly as I could. I knew what it was like to feel fear as a child and all through growing up, and it wasn't something children should experience, so I automatically wanted to get them away from these awful episodes.

Steve was starting to ask Eric about our relationship, asking what his intentions were, and telling him not to mess me about, and that Eric should just leave if that was the case. Eric had Vera on at him as well, telling him he should find a woman with loads of money – in fact, she even arranged a date with her neighbour's daughter, who was a solicitor! Vera told him he was 'jumping out of the frying pan, into the fire with that one!' referring to me, of course. She told him, *"You don't want to be with her, she's like the rest of that family – just look at Steve with Pat!"* How dare she say those things about me, especially the bit about me being the same as the others in my family? That was the worst insult she could have thrown at me – I'm definitely nothing like them!

It seemed to me that, between Pat and Steve, and Eric's mom, they were trying to split us apart: Pat and Steve because they'd lose their live-in nanny, cook, cleaner and general dogsbody if Eric and I got our own place together, and Vera because she didn't want to lose her 'number one son' as she called him. The final straw came when Pat hadn't spoken a single word to me all day while Eric was at work, but, the minute he came home, she cooked steak, chips, peas and mushrooms with onion gravy, for everyone – everyone, that is, except me. I didn't like steak anyway, but I was absolutely sick and tired of being treated like dirt and having her play these mind games, messing with my head.

That night, when we were alone at last in our room, I told Eric I couldn't take any more of this and I was so upset and defeated, I cried for ages. I hadn't done anything to deserve this treatment and it was really hurtful to be on the receiving end. This was such a horrible way to have to live. We agreed that we needed to sort out some different living arrangements and so, as soon as we could, we spoke to my other sister, Diane, and she said we could stay with her for a while. Before I became Pat's skivvy, Diane had held that same unhappy position – until she finally managed to get away and she ran off.

It was a Saturday morning and Steve was taking Pat to work, so I asked him if he would take Hayley with him. Craig was playing outside so I started packing my clothes and personal belongings, but leaving behind anything Pat had bought, or things we'd been sharing, like the hairdryer. Eric and I were just leaving when Craig came in. I explained to him where we were going and I asked him to say goodbye to Hayley for me. I knew that, if I'd seen her, I wouldn't have been able to leave.

We stayed at Diane's for a couple of weeks, during which time I kept getting abusive calls from Pat, calling me a slag and threatening me. She said she'd tell Dad I was on the pill. This was really pathetic, seeing as I was nineteen years old! I had only ever slept with Eric and I was on the pill under medical supervision because my years of controlling my food and not eating from one day to the next, had damaged my body and the pill was to regulate my periods. So, Pat's attempts at hurting me with any of these attacks weren't even valid.

All in all, with not having anywhere permanent to live, the abuse from Pat, and Eric's equally abusive attacks from his ex-wife, we made the decision to pack up and leave the Midlands. In fact, we agreed we'd get away completely, go abroad, and we'd try to find work for both of us so we could stay there. Even then, Vera just had to keep some control and she suddenly announced that she and Eric's dad would come with us, 'to have a holiday' so I couldn't really do or say anything. And so, in less than a year of being together, we got on a plane with Eric's mom and dad, and flew to Ibiza. This was Friday, the thirteenth of May. This was our first holiday abroad, whereas Eric's parents would normally have two foreign holidays a year.

The journey from the airport to the apartment complex in Port des Torrent, just outside San Antonio, was nerve-wracking. We were driven in a coach that had wooden seats, in the pitch black night along unlit dirt track roads and the driver was going way too fast. Let's just say we were glad when we arrived at the apartments.

When we got up on the first morning, Eric suggested going for a walk, and we set off to explore, following along a rough track, through a field and then into San Antonio. At first, we thought this looked like a nice clean place but, when we started walking along the streets to find somewhere to get a drink, we saw that everywhere was awash with dead cockroaches. There had been a recent infestation and this was before San Antonio became a popular tourist area.

The apartment was nice, each block had its own pool, and we were fully self-catering, but we would eat out most of the time and only have snacks in the apartment. One night, when we were out having our evening meal, Vera had one of her 'asthma attacks' – the ones Eric said she would fake when she wasn't getting enough attention – and she asked Eric to take her back to the apartment, leaving me with his dad. Eric managed to get her to go to bed and then he tried to come away but Vera was insisting he stay with her all evening. Eric knew, without a doubt, that she was putting it on and wasn't ill at all, so he didn't go along with her demands this time, and came back to join us. His dad had a bit of a go at him, telling him 'not to be so soft with her' and he said he was going to have a word with her. I knew Vera was trying to break us up, so that she could keep her 'baby boy' with her, however pathetic that seemed. I was fed up of her treating me badly – I'd had all this from Pat and now her, and I really didn't feel I deserved any of it.

The next day it was obvious Vera had been 'told off' because she wasn't speaking to me (again). Eric and I went off to ask around to see if we could find any jobs, but we didn't come up with anything so we just decided to have a really good holiday. We weren't really too bothered, because we had peace of mind, knowing our plan now was to have this holiday, go back home and move to Devon. It didn't take us too long to get in the mood, away from all the bad stuff back home, and soon I was trying all these different drinks that Eric and his dad were giving me. I decided I liked Tia Maria and so I stuck with that, but there was no way I could have known this is not a drink you have a lot of! Eric's dad had only ever seen me as 'quiet little Dawn' so he thought it would be funny to get me drunk. At the end of the evening, I stood up to go back to our room – and promptly fell in a heap! Eric had to carry me to bed, but I spent the rest of the night in the bathroom with my head in the toilet, being very sick. In the morning, my head was banging after being so bad all night. Eric took a photo so he could show me how bad I'd been – for my own good! But I didn't need to be reminded of how that had felt and it wasn't something I'd ever want to repeat.

> *This was my first – and my one and only – experience of getting very drunk, and paying the price! Eric thought it was funny, but it felt so bad, it wasn't funny for me. I suppose he'd seen so much of that kind of thing when he worked at the nightclub, and, being older than me, he'd been around so much more than me. I am now completely a non-drinker, tee-total, and I really hate the thought of being sick ever again.*

Sitting by the pool the next day was torture for my head, especially as it was supposed to be the hottest day for some time, and it was quite embarrassing for me to see Jim again, the chap at the Safari Bar below the apartment – the place where I'd disgraced myself! He teased me, telling me I kept slipping off my bar stool and giggling, and I wasn't sure if he was making it up or not. I just told myself that would never happen *ever again*.

I soon forgot my hangover when the local children came to the pool to play, and with them was a lady whose little girl was wearing a traditional dress and she was dancing – she was beautiful with big blue eyes and a huge smile... I was watching children play...

Chapter eight

New place, new start

Leaving the sunshine and holidaymakers behind on Ibiza, we came back home but, within a couple of weeks, we were off again, this time to move to Torquay. We literally packed our bags, got on a coach and 'rode off into the sunset', as they say. We hadn't planned or organised anything, so we had no idea where we would stay, we had no friends or contacts there, and neither of us had a job to go to – but we had each other and that was all we needed.

As we clambered off the coach in the Lymington Road bus station in Torquay, the first thing we saw was a row of guest houses just across the road and we walked over to them. We both liked the look of one in particular – a big powder blue and white house that had a sort of homely feel to it. We knocked on the door and it was opened by a tall, slim, elderly man wearing a slouchy cable-knit V-neck cardigan that was almost the same blue as the outside paintwork.

He had a roll-up cigarette stuck to his bottom lip, and he introduced himself as Harold, completing the picture of a scene from *Steptoe and Son*, creating an image I will never forget.

Harold called through to the living room, to his wife, Doreen, a little plump lady with a huge smiling face, who came toddling out to greet us. I knew straight away that these were good people, and I knew we'd be happy here. We were shown to our room at the top of the first flight of stairs: when the door opened, I couldn't help but laugh – the room was decorated in the same powder blue!

Over breakfast the next morning, Harold chatted to us, asking what our plans were for our new life in Torquay. We told him we wanted to find jobs and somewhere permanent to stay. He handed us the local paper so we could look at the ads for jobs, and, after breakfast, he very kindly took us down to the Job Centre. When we got back from our job hunting, there was a lovely surprise waiting for us: Harold and Doreen offered us their caravan that was sited in the back garden. It had gas, electricity and water, and they were only asking for a very reasonable rent. This was a great start to our new life, thanks to meeting such lovely, kind people.

Within a couple of weeks, we had three jobs between us! Eric started working at the Babbacombe Pottery and I had two part-time jobs – I worked for Elizabeth Arden in the Argos store in the mornings, and in the afternoons I worked at Ye Olde Coffee and Bakery Shop on Union Street. My new day started with getting up at six-thirty each morning to start work at the coffee shop, popping home after my shift to prepare the dinner for that evening, then going back to town for my afternoon at Argos. Life was busy but I loved it and, although I didn't realise it at the time, having such a full life kept me from thinking too much. I used this as a coping tool until I eventually had a complete burn-out.

Life carried on like this for a few months until Harold had to get rid of the caravan, when he moved us in to the house to live with him, Doreen and their family. We would all sit together in the lounge, watching the telly, we'd cook meals together, sit and eat together, and go on shopping trips together to Trago Mills, a huge factory outlet that sold everything you could think of but was more like a large warehouse. This was what a real family was like, and we both loved it. Sometimes we'd all sit and talk, and we'd play tricks on each other and have some real belly-laughing sessions until the tears were streaming down my cheeks and my ribs ached. Harold had so many party tricks and I remember clearly how he'd haul himself up the inside of the door frame and turn right over, landing back on the floor on his feet. He was a master at this trick until he bought some new trainers and these got stuck on the door frame, with Harold ending up thudding down on the floor. Eric picked him up and made sure he was OK, and Doreen sat there, cussing him for his stupidity – this wasn't real cursing because Doreen didn't swear, it was just playful banter. We carried on laughing about this for days after that, because Harold had sprained his groin and Doreen got him a tube of some sort of cream to rub into the painful area. It was one of those heat rubs and, instead of relieving the situation, it just made him burn! It was probably as painful as the fall was in the first place.

Another of Harold's stunts was to run down the last flight of stairs as fast as he could. One day, we were all sat in the lounge and down he came, waving at us as he ran, but then he tripped on the carpet and kept hurtling forward. He couldn't stop and carried on, right out the open front door and into the street. He was a real character, very funny and so kind. All the guests took to him and he was loved by everybody.

During our time in Torquay, Eric's mom and dad came to visit. As soon as they arrived, Vera started trying to take over with her demands. She wanted Eric to take her into town and show her round the shops, she wanted him to take her to the pubs, to show her the general area, the place where he worked in fact, anything and everything she could think of, to keep him with her and away from me. She'd never wanted him to move away from the Midlands, and, of course, was blaming me. We were getting ready to go out one evening with

Harold and Doreen's son and daughter, Vince and Sharon, when Vera insisted that Eric went to the pub with her for a meal, because *"I've travelled all this way to come and see you..."* and so on. I wanted us to keep to the original plan but Eric went out with his mom and dad, leaving me to get ready to go out with the others. I was really upset that Eric had left me to go on my own, and Doreen was really sympathetic, hugging me and trying to console me. She said I should go out with Vince and Sharon anyway, and not let Vera see that she'd spoiled everything, not let her have the pleasure of knowing she'd upset me. Doreen taught me to be strong in ways I hadn't known before, she accepted me, encouraged me and – most importantly – she made me realise I was allowed to stand up for myself.

Eric's mom was always very controlling and not a nice person, but his dad, also called Eric, was a lovely man, good-looking with long, dark, wavy hair and steely blue eyes that sparkled. He used to shout at Vera when she started telling her terrible lies. He could be funny, too, but not as funny as Harold.

Later that same evening, after I'd made it clear to Eric that I wasn't happy with him dumping me for his mom, and I told him I would never do that to him, I said he needed to stand up for himself because I couldn't do it for him all the time. Eric wasn't at all confident and if he needed to ask for something in a shop, I'd be the one to ask; if he needed an appointment with the doctor or anything like that, I'd be the one to make the call, and so on. He wasn't the big, strong man that he portrayed with his weight trainer image from the gym.

When Eric's parents had gone back to the Midlands, life was once more happy with our new friends who were more like our family. Sometimes, a guest would try to avoid paying their bill and Eric would be called in to throw them out, or, if guests were too noisy and disrespectful, Eric would send them on their way. Once, Vince had been to a party and had had a few too many to drink, and he fell asleep in the bathroom. This was the bathroom Harold had painted in bright aquamarine. I'm convinced, if he'd woken up in there, the colour alone would have made him ill! Eric had to try to break the lock off the door and get Vince back to his bed, which he did eventually manage, but it took ages because he had to be careful not to disturb the guests.

The time came when we decided to find a place of our own and we moved into a flat over a Chinese restaurant on Upper Union Street. A friend of ours, a girl called Julie, had got herself a job at the local swimming baths complex and we'd agreed she could come and stay with us when we found somewhere. It wasn't as nice as being at Harold and Doreen's, but I scrubbed it clean and then decorated with some tins of paint I found in the cupboard under the sink and that made it much better. We settled in, Julie moved in, and I carried on doing my morning shift, popping to the flat to get dinner ready then going off to do the afternoon job. After a while, the girl who was managing the coffee shop just upped and left without any notice and I was asked to take over her job full-time, which I was happy to do.

We did visit back home regularly while we lived in Torquay, hiring a car that Eric would drive, and there was always some family battle or other while we were there. Once, we visited while Mom and Dad were looking after Hayley and, when I saw her, I went to give her a hug but she moved away from me, telling me her mom and dad would hit her if she came near me. As she spoke, I could see the fear in her face, and it left me cold. I could see myself as a child like her, but, because I wasn't around any more, I wouldn't be able to protect her. Another example of manipulation and cruelty to a child. When Steve came to collect Hayley, Dad hit the roof for that, but I kept out of the way, crying round the back of the house. All I'd done was leave home, but you'd have thought I'd committed a terrible crime. I cried all the way back to Devon.

Another time when we went to visit Eric's mom and dad, there was a phone call from Pat and she asked Vera if she could speak to me to ask if we could make friends again, but Vera said no. At this, my stubbornness took over – I wasn't going to have Vera speaking for me! I was livid and, on the way back from theirs, I asked Eric to drop me to the bookie's in Rushall where Pat was working. She saw me and came out to meet me, then she gave me a hug – but she never apologised for calling me names, for the accusations, for stopping Hayley talking to me… NOT ONE SINGLE THING. So, we just brushed all of the real issues aside, without resolving anything, as always. I should have learned my lesson, but I was too naïve.

On every visit, Eric was faced with fighting to get his divorce. The court had been trying to serve legal papers on Tracey but, as expected, she wasn't co-operating at all, and they could never find her to hand her the documents. She really thought Eric would go back to her at some point.

Back in Torquay again, and at least this time, I was allowed to ring and speak to Hayley. But, each time I called, she would become very emotional, crying on the phone and asking me to go back. Being so far away, this was really upsetting for me and I was missing her as much as she was missing me but, much worse than this, I knew that, if she was being left alone down my mom's, what was to stop Derek doing something to her? Who was there to keep an eye on him? I was afraid for Hayley and I was also afraid for my own state of mind. I had my nice new life with Eric, and with Harold and Doreen as the most caring parental figures, but poor Hayley was left in the most vulnerable position and that was a heavy burden for me.

Eventually, Eric was made redundant from the

pottery, and – although he was reinstated in a different job there – this was when Dad became seriously ill and my worries over Hayley were really taking hold, so we decided it was for the best to go back to the Midlands. We stayed in Torquay for about two years altogether, and this period of time included me reaching my twenty-first birthday.

Steve drove down to collect us and Hayley came with him, while Eric's mom and dad came in their car to fetch our belongings back, and we all stayed together that night at Kingskerwell holiday caravan site. Julie, Eric and I had all given up our jobs but Julie had been given some free tickets for the swimming complex, so it was decided we'd all spend some time there the following day before setting off. That evening, Eric and Julie both said they weren't really bothered about going and I'd never wanted to go, mainly because I wouldn't wear a swimsuit or show my body in public – another long-term result of the childhood abuse. When Eric told Vera in the morning that we wouldn't be going, she immediately turned on me, cursing me, accusing me, blaming me, *"It's all your fault!"* even though I was trying to explain to her that it really wasn't my fault. She just wouldn't listen and I was back to being that child again, being victimised for something that wasn't down to me, something I had no control over. She threw her arm out to belt me as I heard Eric's dad say *"Vera, bloody leave her alone!"* But it was too late – she caught me a blow as I was stepping out of the caravan door. The attack, and the sudden pain, shocked me and I felt hurt and upset. All I could think to say was *"You big fat cow!"* and, even then, I was scared to swear or to be rude in case she would tell my dad. Some would call this respect, but I call it fear.

I took myself off and went to sit in the launderette, then Hayley appeared, running in to tell me, *"Nan said she curses your wedding and Tracey was better than you!"* Tracey being Eric's first wife, the person Vera had never been able to say a good word about, and who she'd referred to as 'an old slag'. I was crying now, and shaking with the shock of everything, and Hayley was hugging me, trying to comfort me. She declared loudly, *"I hate my nanny!"* Despite everything, I told Hayley she shouldn't be nasty about Vera, saying she was probably just tired from all the travelling. Always the peacemaker.

When it came to teatime, Vera sent Eric's dad to Babbacombe chip shop to get fish and chips for everyone. When the food arrived, there was a meal for everyone else, but not for me. This took me back to how Pat would treat me when I lived with her. Of course, the others offered me some of their food but I was too stubborn and wouldn't give Vera the satisfaction of seeing me eat anything she'd provided, anything she had control over. I went hungry but was used to this because it had become a way to punish myself through all the hiccups in my life. I would control food by only eating when I was really hungry. It was my control.

It was a quiet night in the caravan but Julie, Eric and me were soon able to find some humour in Vera's attack on me, and we started chanting, *"It's a knockout… in one!"* and *"It's Vera in the caravan and Dawn splattered up the door…"* I bet Vera was really peed off with us laughing about it, but I knew Eric's dad wouldn't let her come out of that room, even if she'd wanted to.

The following morning, we packed the cars up but Vera had decided she wouldn't travel with anything of mine in their car, so Julie and all her belongings had to go in their car, instead of with us in Steve's. It was hard to tell who was the child in the group – Hayley or Vera!

Once we were back home, Eric's divorce became final and he was free at last. He came out of the courthouse and went straight round the corner to the Registrar's office, where he made the booking for our wedding. The date was to be the twenty-eighth of October, 1989.

Eric's divorce was really messy, with Tracey causing every problem she could. First, she'd let him see the kids, then she'd suddenly change her mind and he wouldn't be able to have them again. The court ordered Eric to pay her six pounds a week but the judge said, if it was up to him, he'd make Tracey pay because of the way she behaved throughout the proceedings. Weekend and holiday visits with the children were also ordered. Coming out of the courthouse, Eric tried to give the children some money and Tracey was shouting at him, saying this was 'guilt money' because he *"… took off down Devon so nobody could find you!"* She really didn't want the divorce because Eric had always been a good dad and a good provider for the family, whereas her new partner was in prison for stealing from the company he worked for.

Chapter nine

Building a new family, a new life

The day came, and Eric and I were married.

> We had agreed we wanted the wedding to be simple – no fuss, no frills. But, once again, as it got closer to the date, Pat took over and started making all the arrangements. I was happy to be marrying Eric, happy that my lovely Hayley was to be my bridesmaid, and nothing else mattered, so I sat back and let Pat do as she pleased.

Even on the way to the Registrar's office, my dad was still trying to convince me I didn't have to 'go through with it' – as if marrying my perfect man was some kind of torture! He told me married men always go back to their wives, which I thought was a bit silly because Dad knew what a miserable time Eric had had with his first wife, but then I realised he was probably thinking about his own situation, not mine and Eric's. Dad's affair had lasted a long time, and had even produced two children, and yet he'd never left Mom and the family.

As it has turned out, our marriage has been bliss. Apart from the bits where my family have interfered! But, even with all of their goings-on, it has served to make us stronger, which is exactly the opposite of what they were trying to achieve.

It seemed as if they all took it in turns to attack us, to cause problems that were their problems but they needed us to see them as ours, to try to drag us into their world. But it was a world we didn't belong in, and this is how life turns such things around because all they managed to do was to make us stronger, make us realise, over and over again, that our place was not with them, make us appreciate the life we had built together.

We'd have Vera, as always, doing her best (worst) to get under my skin and to pull Eric away; Pat and Hayley would argue and fight constantly and they would try to pull me in to whatever the latest problem was; every now and again, Diane would try to turn Dad against Eric by telling him Eric was treating me really badly; Micky would turn up at our house late at night for a visit because he never worked and so he slept for most of the day; George would come to us when he was in a bad state, either drunk or drugged up; Nigel would turn up drunk and, whenever he was in trouble with the law, he'd ask to be bailed to our address. There were two reasons for this request: one, because Mom and Dad thought there was more chance of me being able to get through to Nigel, to talk some sense into him, and, two, because we hadn't got a reputation with the police like the rest of my family had, so there would be more chance of the bail being granted. Then there was all the lies and deceit – they would all want me to cover for them if I wanted them to accept me.

On top of all this, Derek was now married with his own family and I was looking after his disabled child, being involved to the point of helping to get them a new house that had been adapted for disabled use, and then I went round to do painting and decorating, to make the place more comfortable. This was something Eric couldn't understand or accept, seeing me being civil to Derek and helping his family, but even this didn't really get between us. I just knew I needed to find myself – to find *me* – before I could accept myself and everything life had been throwing at me.

Once, Pat had an argument with Eric over something he had dared to say when her dog had bitten a child who was visiting Pat's house. The boy was with his family and they came to Pat and Steve's a couple of times a year from their home in Norwich. So the boy had been there before, and met the dog, played with it and so on. It's not as if the dog didn't know him. The boy was walking past an open door, carrying his drink on his way outside, and this dog just pounced on him. Earlier, the boy had been sitting with the dog, stroking it, so this came as a real shock, and the dog went for his face. The outcome could have easily been really dreadful and Eric was right to comment. This dog was a cross between a pug and a Jack Russell, one of the many Dad had bred, one of the many Hayley had begged her granddad to let her have and he'd given them to her. Every time Hayley brought another dog home, Pat would get rid of it. This one was an unpredictable animal – it liked to be close to people and would sit on top of the cushion behind your neck and head when you sat in an armchair. Then, if you tried to shift it, it would growl and snarl at you.

When Pat created this argument with Eric, I was pregnant with Charlie at the time and I really didn't need the stress, so Eric and I left after her outburst and we went back home. This time, Pat said she wasn't speaking to either of us – as usual, this meant me, not Eric. I decided I needed to keep my distance. Never one to get the message and let anything go, Pat then organised a meal at a local pub and, as usual, we were 'summoned' and we went along. There was Pat and Steve; Craig and his wife, Nqocly (Craig's wife's family are Chinese and this is her given name, but we call her Noc for short); Hayley; Ronnie's son, Ronald; and me and Eric. We sat through the meal together and everyone chatted, and there was never a word from Pat about the latest fall-out, not one word of apology or admission of anything she'd done wrong. And so, life carried on again.

On the eighteenth of April, 1996, I gave birth to our son, Charlie. A fine, healthy baby, bringing so much joy to our lives. Hayley was with me in the car on the way to the hospital and she thought she'd be able to stay with me all through the birth – after all, she was my little shadow and she was with me every minute she could be.

When Charlie was two years old, we lost my dad to lung cancer, only twelve weeks after him being diagnosed. It was strange that he died on exactly the same date as Eric's dad had passed away some years earlier.

Some friends were going to visit a clairvoyant and I went along with them – more for fun than anything serious – and this lady told me she could see a new baby, a boy. I laughed and told her *'Well, I definitely wasn't pregnant when I walked in here!'* but she went on to say that a man who was having breathing difficulties was holding his chest, and he was watching over this baby boy who was very poorly. She did make a point of adding that this was nothing to worry about and the baby was going to be fine. I know it's easy for anyone to make some personal connection to these things, but my dad did have his heart problems and then lung cancer.

Not long after this, I was pregnant and, on the twenty-third of December, 2001, little Harry came into our world. More joy.

At just eighteen months of age, Harry was rushed to hospital suffering from pneumococcal septicaemia and he had gone into anaphylactic shock. He had been poorly and I'd taken him to see the doctor earlier, who told me it was just a cold. He was a bit cranky and wouldn't take his drinks properly, and I thought he must be teething: I did check him over and there was no rash or spots anywhere. Eric went out and I started getting Harry bathed and into his nightclothes, ready for bed but, when I tried to give him his bottle, he wouldn't take it and by now there was obviously something wrong.

I decided to ring the NHS Helpline, which was relatively new at the time, thinking I could get some advice, but the nurse I spoke to insisted on sending an ambulance right away, even when I offered to take him in myself in the car. She kept me talking on the phone, describing Harry's condition and she explained how I should lay him on the floor in a certain way until the ambulance arrived – which it did incredibly quickly and little Charlie, who was being very brave, answered the door to let the paramedics in while I sat with Harry. Within seconds, we were in the ambulance, racing to Walsall Manor hospital. I hadn't even thought about meningitis because Harry had no rash, but, the minute we arrived at the hospital, two tiny spots appeared in his groin. Less than four hours after being seen by the local doctor, little Harry was critical and was fighting for his life.

All through this, I felt Harry would be safe, that he was in the right place and was being taken care of in the best possible way. Strangely, instead of feeling scared, I stayed calm. I thought, even if they can't save him, I know they will have tried their very best and that's all there can be. Thank heaven, Harry did pull through. He's a fighter, just like his mom!

We will always be deeply indebted to everyone involved in Harry's care – from the NHS Helpline operator to the ambulance staff and the hospital nurses and doctors, with a special mention for the Egyptian doctor who was on call that night and who was so quick to diagnose the condition and administer the antibiotics. They all played a part in saving our child's life.

The two boys, Charlie and Harry, are very different. Charlie is quiet, reserved, diplomatic and clever, whereas Harry is fiery, strong-willed, very opinionated and clever, but inventive with it. Between Eric and me, we've made sure that both of our boys have had a *very* different upbringing from the ones we had. They are encouraged to question things, to voice their own opinions and ideas, to express their thoughts, and they are allowed the freedom to be what *they* want to be, to be who *they* want to be. And they are very much loved and cuddled every day.

For my part, I have instilled in them the principle that family does not have to be through the bloodline, but it can be whoever they choose it to be, whoever they want in their lives. If I have one regret in my life with my boys, it is that I have held them back at times because of my own past experiences.

Eric and the boys have certainly kept me going over the years and they are, without doubt, the most important people in my life. Our boys make me so proud to be their mom, and I am blessed with them both. I believe that meeting Eric was meant to be, and that he came into my life to save me and protect me. The love we have is very strong and has survived, regardless of all the attempts by others to damage or destroy it. I wouldn't change anything about Eric – except maybe I'd like him to have his dad's sparkly blue eyes then he'd be my perfect gent! We share a lot of fun, teasing each other and joking around, and we can laugh *at* each other as well as *with* each other, which keeps our friendship alive, as well as our love for each other and for our boys, whatever life puts in front of us.

Chapter ten

Eric's lost children

We carried on for several years, picking Eric's children up so he could spend some time with them, but Tracey didn't want me there, so Eric and his dad would go for them. When Eric started working shifts and couldn't always be around to collect them – and especially if Tracey wanted to go out for the weekend – then it was suddenly OK for me to be there. While we lived in our one-bedroom flat, we could only have the children in the daytime, but there would inevitably be times when we would take them back to her place and there would be no-one there, no matter how many times we tried going back. On these occasions, we'd give the children our bed and we'd sleep on the floor. Tracey often sent the kids asking for money for clothes, but we were wise to this and we'd buy them something to wear, rather than risk any money being spent on drink. Many times we'd find the children had been left overnight with a 'babysitter' who was barely old enough to look after themselves, never mind two younger children. We hated to see all of this going on and it really bothered us when we had to take them back, so we eventually contacted the social services to see if they could help.

This resulted in a visit by a male social worker, who told us it was OK for the children to be left, as long as they could find some food and make a drink for themselves – in fact, a six-year-old could stay with a three-year-old if they weren't in danger from fire or boiling water! We were amazed to hear this but it was the law so we couldn't do anything. This chap said he would keep us informed but he was due to be away from work to have some surgery so we wouldn't hear from him for some time. We made countless calls after this but we never heard another word. Another failure by 'the system', more gaping holes in a shockingly inadequate service – even after we had reported and complained about the children being left alone, having to take themselves to school, being left to stand on the doorstep in all weathers if no-one was home, and two small children – one eight years old and the other five – playing truant from school. No-one seemed to care.

Tracey went on to have two more children around the time I had Charlie and then we were able to see more of Eric's two, but it seemed we were only in favour whenever we were paying for everything, like the trip to Majorca when we paid for their passports, new clothes, the entire holiday and all spending money. As they grew into their teenage years, we never really saw much of them because they had found their own feet and had their own friends and independence.

> *I find it very sad that Eric's children don't even acknowledge their dad's birthday – not even a simple card – or a Christmas card or message. Nothing. It's heartbreaking. He will say it's because he wasn't there for them when they were young, but that's not the true picture, as I know only too well. He wasn't given the chance to be a dad to them, and I know he's a great dad because Charlie and Harry both adore him.*

Chapter eleven

The beginning of the end

It was 2007, and Eric's aunt, a truly beautiful lady who had been more of a mother to him than Vera ever was, sadly passed away. She had been poisoned against me and Eric by Pat and Steve, Eric's older brother, Mick, and Vera, having been told some terrible things – all lies – so we didn't see her, or hear from her, for a very long time. Some years later, when her husband had died, they brought her back to the Midlands to live with Vera and she came to visit us in our home and she saw for herself our little family unit, and how close and happy we were. She wanted to visit us more, but Vera and her clan wouldn't let her. This upset Eric greatly because he was so fond of her.

Less than twelve months from her moving in with Vera, she was taken ill and was in bed, but Vera didn't believe her and made her get up, at which the poor lady collapsed with a massive stroke. As she lay in the hospital bed after her passing, Eric was heartbroken, but his mother and brothers showed no remorse whatsoever, and Steve and Mick were eager to get back home to clear away every trace of her, which was all to do with her Will.

This lady was no relation to Steve and Pat, but there was Pat, telling me we shouldn't try to find the aunt's only son, and asking me to keep quiet until the Will was read. Pat actually told me I could have a share of the money from the aunt's Will, which, by the way, had been changed in April of the same year as she died in the September. Eric made the point that the son *should* be found and told of his mother's death, and he also said the Will should be given proper examination, and that he would ask Mick for a copy of it. When this turned up, the son's name had been blacked out with a permanent marker pen and the beneficiaries were, surprise, surprise, Mick and Vera.

Eric couldn't come to terms with the loss of this lovely lady, nor could he take the callousness of the others, and when the offer of money was brought up, Eric asked me to go to Birmingham to get a copy of the Will as it was before the changes were made, which we assumed would have the son's name on it and we could start to search for him before the funeral.

By this time, I'd left my job at the bookies in Aldridge, where Pat worked as well, to get away from her controlling ways and the disruption she would cause. I hadn't wanted to leave, because I loved the work and I had made friends with many of the regular customers, but, as usual, it was me backing down to try to get the 'bad rubbish' out of my life.

Pat rang me and I told her to keep the money from the Will, if that's what she wanted, because we didn't want anything to do with it. I said nothing good could ever come out of ill-gotten gains, to which she replied that she would speak to Eric instead, hoping to get him to agree to the offer. This made me even more angry, and my answer came easily, *"If Eric chooses to bring that money into my house, he'll follow it right back out again through the window!"*

> Some time after this happened, Eric said he thought I was more concerned about the mess of my windows than anything else! He always manages to make a joke and pour some light into situations when I need bringing back down from something upsetting me badly, although, at the time, he understood I meant business because I disagreed so strongly with the total lack of moral values being shown by Pat and the others.

It was then that Pat said she wished my boys dead and gone from me. I knew then, in an instant, that this was really the end of our relationship, forever. I said to her, ever so calmly, *"That's fine, don't bother coming here again and if you let me know you're not looking after Mom on Fridays, I'll go and fetch her. I don't want Mom spite because we've fallen out."* Regrettably, Hayley carried on ringing me, every time she and Pat had a row, wanting me to step in and get involved, but I knew now I had to break all contact with Pat, so I told Hayley, *"If you two can't sit down and talk to one another sensibly, then don't talk at all – make your choice because I'm fed up of hearing it."* Hayley obviously took this as a refusal to help her, which is what I'd been doing for all of her life, and she fell out with me. Pat carried on having Mom for a couple of weeks, but, when Hayley and I had this fall-out, she just stopped coming – but she didn't bother to let me know poor Mom was on her own.

Hayley then started a campaign of her own abuse against me, leaving messages on my house phone, calling me a bitch, a slag, saying *"I hate you!"*... anything she could think of to upset me or make me react, and, because I didn't reply to any of this, she began sending text messages that were really horrible. One of these said *"I'll ask Nan about the rape, let's see if it's the truth, and about Derek!"*

Unfortunately, Charlie would check the house answerphone if he saw there was a message, and he'd let me know who had rung and what they'd said, which was absolutely fine. He'd also answer my mobile or pick up my text messages for me – this started because he's quite technical and I'm definitely not, so I was happy for him to do this. Anyway, in our home there was never anything to hide from each other, so none of this was a problem. Until now.

Charlie heard Hayley's voice, spitting out her nasty remarks to me, about me, and then, when he read the text messages as well, he was left feeling very confused about what these comments could possibly mean. He knew I'd always been very close to Hayley, and he knew nothing of what had happened to me in the past. My hand was now being forced and it was sooner than I'd wanted to tell him about these things, but I couldn't have him upset and with no answers – that would have gone against everything I'd taught him. I took him to school, telling him that we would sit down and talk that evening, and that I would explain everything. Charlie idolised Hayley, just as I always had, and now he couldn't understand how cruel she was being, or why.

I tried to ring Hayley but got no answer on either the house phone or her mobile, but she did send me one text, telling me to leave her alone, so I replied to that, asking her *"Was there any need for that?"* My friend, Lisa, came round as we'd planned to go into town with Harry and do some shopping, and I told her what had happened. She was disgusted and she asked me if I'd prefer to stay indoors and not bother with the shops, but I'd promised Harry and it wouldn't be fair to him to change the plans now, so we went to Bloxwich. We went round the shops and then sat in a café for a while, and that's when Hayley rang me on my mobile. I answered and I explained how upset Charlie was at the dreadful picture she had painted of me in her various voice messages and texts, which he was now carrying in his head. I asked her why did she have to say such a cruel thing, because now I had no choice but to tell Charlie things he was a bit too young to hear about, because there was no way I was going to tell him any lies. Hayley apologised to me, saying she'd been upset because I said I didn't want to get involved any longer between her and her mom, with all their arguments and rows. As we were talking, Pat arrived home and Hayley asked me if I'd call her back later, when Pat wouldn't be there. I remember being so calm as I said *"No, I won't be calling you again, or speaking to you, so this is the last time you'll hear from me, but I won't stop you talking to the boys. Bye."*

The tears were rolling down my face as the realisation sank in that I had loved and adored Hayley for all of her life, only to see her to turn into someone the same as the rest of my birth family – evil, wicked, malicious and manipulative. But I also believe that, because she *was* like this, it made it easier for me to break the chain.

Later that same day, when I collected Charlie from school and then Eric came home from work, it was the time when I had to sit an eleven-year-old boy down to tell him about his mom's past life, about the abuse and the rape, all in as gentle and delicate a way as I could, so as not to cause him any more harm. I told him I wasn't sad and that I hoped he wouldn't be, and that sometimes in life, things happen to people that really shouldn't happen but we must never forget those things because they are what makes us who we are. I told him that I had always intended to tell both him and his little brother, but not quite so early in their little lives, and I explained that I had been left with no choice but to tell Charlie now, because of what he had seen and heard. I told him that it was his decision whether he wanted to speak to Pat or Hayley, and I made sure he understood that I wouldn't be upset or angry, whatever he chose to do, because I knew he cared for them both. He was fairly adamant that he wouldn't, ever again. It's not an easy thing to explain to a young child, but I tried to tell him sometimes people say nasty things that they don't really mean, and I mentioned that Hayley had apologised to me and that she was very sorry for what she had said.

I would never have dealt with this by threatening my children to stop talking to Pat and Hayley, the way Pat had done with Hayley when I was visiting from Torquay.

> *It was possibly a good thing that I had to talk to Charlie at this time, because I was always aware that one or another of the family would use this information one day to cause me problems and try to upset my life. There was no way I wanted my sons to hear any of this from them.*

From that day on, I've always encouraged Charlie to talk to me openly and not worry about upsetting me if he has any questions about the abuse or the rape, and I would answer the best I could, without going into too much detail. Charlie, bless him, offered to help me to explain things to Harry when he was older – Charlie didn't think his little brother would be able to take this information as calmly as he had done.

Chapter twelve

Enough is enough

Even when I'd left my job at the bookies to avoid any more upset, Pat still couldn't let things lie and she began following me around, turning up at my work with Hayley, and they would start laughing and making comments about me, for anyone to hear. This went on for weeks, with displays of Pat's unbelievably immature behaviour in these attempts to disrupt my work or maybe get me into trouble, or even just to embarrass me – and all because she had lost her control over me.

One day, I was doing my cleaning job in the bookies in Aldridge and there was Pat, outside the shop, waving her arms around in my direction and laughing. I finished my work and then drove straight to her house and knocked on the front door. When she opened the door, I asked her to stop what she was doing to me and leave me alone. I honestly didn't want anything to do with her but

I had to say this, and I really meant it — I just wanted her to *leave me alone.* She stood there, looking at me, and said *"I don't know what you're talking about, you stupid child!"* then Steve came to the door and he joined in, telling Pat to *"Come on in away from the silly little stupid bitch."* This was like a red rag to a bull and I let him have it, telling him he was nothing more than a paedophile who had raped his own sister then blamed her for everything, because they said she was drunk.

Shaun was sitting in the car, waiting for me. He would come with me when I was doing late cleaning jobs after the night racing had finished, just to make sure I was safe. I had told him to stay in the car because this wasn't his argument, but Pat started shouting abuse at him, telling him to 'watch your back!' because he was still speaking to me. But Steve had to go one further and he pulled his trousers down, shouting over to Shaun *"D'you want a bit of this?"* which was his way of taunting Shaun for being gay. Shaun threw himself out of the car and headed for the house, but Pat and Steve slammed the door shut, luckily. They knew, as well as I did, Shaun could have a bit of a temper.

I dragged Shaun away and we got back in the car. I drove to the police station, determined that it was high time something was done *officially* about this 'family' of mine. I told the police about Pat's behaviour towards me, how she was following me around, hassling me at my work, taunting me and constantly making my life a misery... The police weren't bothered because it was a 'domestic' matter, as they put it – there was no stalking, no harassment, no bullying... Maybe it was the fact that I had *finally* gone to someone for help, someone who was official, in a position to *do something*, not just to listen like a friend, and they were telling me they couldn't (wouldn't?) do anything about it; maybe that was the final straw, after all the years of being controlled, being hurt, being abused, and being ignored, not having a voice... Whatever it was that tipped the scales, this was the point in time when I stood up and told the world I was having no more of it. I had found my voice and *no-one* was going to keep me quiet, not any more.

I'd had enough now. Enough of all of it – the bullying, the control, the lies and deceit – and I spoke to the police about the sexual abuse from Derek when I was young, I told them about being raped by Diane's ex-boyfriend, and about the never-ending hassle I'd had from Pat, which was what had driven me to be there in the first place. I told them I was bringing all of this out into the open so nobody could hold anything over me ever again, so nobody could throw any of it in my face at every opportunity.

> *When I lived in Dryden Road and Diane had come to my house, shouting her mouth off and calling me all the terrible names she could put*

> her tongue to, I had gone down to Mom and Dad's house, fully intending to come clean to Dad about the abuse. But I let myself be talked out of doing it by Mom and Sean Wayne because Mom was scared of what Dad would do. What about me? What about how I felt? I could have ended it all there and then if they had let me.

For some reason, Diane was with me when I went to the police and, to this day, I've no idea why she was there, because we hadn't spoken for years, since she told Hayley that Craig wasn't her real brother. Anyway, there we both were, and the police arranged interviews for me and for Diane, and this is when it came out that Derek had abused her as well. After our interviews, the police planned to interview family members and any friends who I'd confided in as I was growing up, and these interviews would take place before they arrested Derek and David. I had to have regular contact with the police liaison officers dealing with the case, but I couldn't help getting upset every time I spoke to them. I'd always made it clear that I didn't want anybody to go to jail – all I ever wanted was an apology, for them both to admit to their crimes and then we could all get on with our lives, just like I'd been doing for all of these years.

The police were happy to carry their investigations forward with the Child Protection Unit in Bloxwich, but the Crown Prosecution

Service in Wolverhampton declined the case because it was historic and they were aware that the court would probably see Derek now as the 'caring father' looking after his disabled child, a real pillar of the community, and this would most definitely cause them to feel sympathy for him, especially as the abuse was so far in the past, and, in a household of two adults and eleven children, nobody could tell the police anything at all useful and nobody had seen or heard anything, according to them. I accepted this but Diane wanted justice, payback, and she wasn't going to give in. She asked to see the people who were 'playing with her life' and we both went to the CPS offices in Wolverhampton with the female police officers who were dealing with us, to demand some answers. Diane asked for copies of the statements, but I didn't see the point in having a copy for myself, because there was no way we could change the outcome. It wouldn't make any difference in helping me come to terms with what I already knew deep down – that nobody could tell the truth in those statements, so I left the matter there.

The CPS made the point to me that I hadn't mentioned David when I was interviewed, and my reply to this was to try to explain that, all through my childhood, I was only allowed to speak when I was spoken to and that I was constantly controlled by fear, always under threat of awful things happening to me or to those I loved. When you have been conditioned in this way, even when you reach your adult years, you don't speak out easily, you only give out information when you are questioned, and the police hadn't asked me about David. Alongside this, I really had no wish to see either Derek or David jailed, so I was probably not being as free with my information as I might otherwise have been.

We were each assigned Victim Support and they arranged a claim for compensation for us both, from which Diane received sixteen thousand pounds, but my claim was declined. I wasn't looking for any money from this, so I wasn't bothered. My support worker, however, contested the decision against my claim and I was subsequently awarded the same amount as Diane, but I knew I couldn't accept it or have anything whatsoever to do with it. Of course, everyone had an idea as to what I should do with this large amount of money… my brother, Sean Wayne, told me to use it to pay off some of the mortgage or give it to the boys, others told me to keep it (those who don't know the real me, DAWN). But Eric, Lisa, Shaun and Wayne understood when I said I could have absolutely no connection with this money, because it was linked directly to the abuse, to all of the pain and the fear, to the rape… If I'd used it for the mortgage, I'd have felt like those perpetrators had bought me, and my happy home would be tarnished with those memories. I made my decision to donate the whole lot to charity, and to move on.

After my hand was forced to go to the police, I found out exactly what my birth family were all like for real, and everything I'd thought about them over the years suddenly jumped up and hit me hard in the face. When they were interviewed to find out if any of them knew anything about what I claimed had taken place, they all said they had told the police what they knew about Derek – more lies! Brenda said Derek had abused her and that she had told the police. She said she knew she should have protected me – if she hadn't known anything at the time, why should she need to protect me? Mom said she didn't know anything about the abuse until I told her recently when I first went to the police. She was obviously forgetting that day in the kitchen when she'd asked me if Derek was doing anything to me and I told her he was 'shagging' me. Shaun said he could only tell the police what he knew, which was next to nothing. Mickey said Diane had previously accused him, which didn't help my case, but was he just covering his own back because he was still sharing a room with Derek? Sean Wayne said he told the police about Derek hanging around with convicted paedophiles and that he always thought Derek was 'a strange 'un' ... Everyone else said they knew absolutely nothing. I found all of this out when I read their statements much later. What else did I expect from my birth family, except lies and deception, protecting themselves and trying to cover up what had been going on in the family home – the house of horrors in the true sense.

> Because the only thing I ever wanted was for Derek and David to apologise to me for what they had done, I wrote a letter to each of them before the police involvement and again, afterwards. Neither of them has ever bothered to give me their apology. I have forgiven both of them for what they did to me, but an apology would have shown me they felt some remorse, and that would have given me closure.

My health wasn't too good around this time, due to bouts of vomiting every day which were being caused by hormonal problems. After several investigations, my consultant decided I should have a hysterectomy, which would free me from the constant sickness. This was seen by Pat and Steve, Mick and Vera as yet another opportunity to have a go at me, and they would taunt me as they passed by Mom's house. They told Sean Wayne I was a 'kooka choo', using this expression as an insult to mean I had gone crazy from hormonal problems, had lost my senses.

I was booked in to the hospital and I went in and had the operation. Once I'd recovered from the surgery, I gave up my cleaning jobs in order to make a fresh start, completely away from the bookies and, hopefully, out of reach of Pat and any other members of my birth family.

Looking through the Current Vacancies adverts in the local paper, one job in particular caught my eye – Civil Enforcement Officer, otherwise known as traffic warden! I sent in my application and was successful, then, after my training, I started patrolling the local areas of the town. This was a job I loved doing, because I was meeting people and was able to talk to them, make contact with them and connect with them – and I was being paid to do it! I did find the uniform was a bit of a barrier at first, but when people saw I was treating them with respect, they realised I was a human being, not just a uniform.

I hadn't been there long before I was offered a manager's position, mainly due to those above me seeing I had people skills, and I was promoted to Team Manager. One of my colleagues, another team manager, was dyslexic and had problems with understanding the office procedures. It was clear to me that no-one else was helping him with this difficulty, but I was very happy to do so. Another of the managers, a chap called Paul, became quite worried that I would progress through the ranks, taking with me the colleague I was helping, and leave him behind, so he started to see me as a threat.

Around this time, a new office manager was appointed, a lady called Harj, who I'd worked with previously on a different contract. Things changed after this, when all the team managers were summoned to a meeting with Harj, who told us that she'd had a meeting with the council – the organisation who were employing us and paying us to do the job – and that she had been instructed to pass on to us that all traffic wardens would be expected to give out one and a quarter tickets every hour on average, meaning they should issue a total of nine tickets every day.

I wasn't happy with this as I could see the pitfalls for everyone concerned, and I made the point to Harj that our officers, the wardens, would be made targets for abuse by the public, plus this would encourage bad practice within the staff, should they fall short of their targets. I knew then that my days were numbered in this job, but I told myself if I carried on doing my work to the best of my ability and remained true to myself by being honest, then I would survive. How very wrong I was.

This is when the campaign against me started. I would arrive at the office to find the keys for the staff mopeds had been moved and hidden, so I couldn't send them out, when I opened the parking barriers, someone would immediately close them again behind me, so the council employees couldn't get in to park their cars at their workplace and lots of complaints would come in; the charging stations used for the wardens' radios and hand-held computers would be turned off; important messages would be held back and not given to me until late in the day when I wouldn't have time to deal with them…

Every day became hell at work, every morning I was walking in to a battle-ground, but I wasn't going to buckle – I'd been through far worse than this. One day, I walked in to find Harj and Paul talking about me and Harj was saying *"I don't fucking care about her rota for the car park – if she ain't happy she knows where the door is!"* When I heard this, I decided I did need to move back down to being a warden again as I didn't see the point in constantly putting up with this, and I gave my notice in to Harj. I was sick of the mind games and the mental fighting every day, but she wouldn't accept my notice and she asked me to think about it.

I didn't need to think about it. I spoke to the area manager about the way I was being treated in the workplace, I contacted the council and I even got in touch with some of the national bullying helplines… but, as usual, no-one was listening and here I was, back in an environment where I was being controlled by someone who, for whatever reasons they believed they might have, wanted to hurt me and cause me problems. In other words – a bully.

This was one too many times.

I knew I was feeling all sorts of bad things – angry, upset, stressed, helpless… but I was actually heading for rock bottom and there wasn't much further down to go. I was so bad, Diane went to speak to the council but they weren't interested because I was only subcontracted – even though the council promoted a no-bullying policy and we all worked under their 'umbrella' policies. Several times, I tried to have mediation and I would return to work, but each time I went back it would all start again with the same two people.

After this, I fell into a deep depression and I sank as far down as a human being can sink. I couldn't get back up. I tried to kill myself. There was no room for me to consider anyone else, I could only see me, could only think about me, and 'me' didn't want to carry on. I was so buried, I'd lost contact with everything in my life. I didn't want to have to keep living as myself... I wanted all the pain, the hurt, the torment, to go away for good...

I went for a walk on my own. There was a big lorry coming along the road and I stepped out in front of it. Just as quickly, I felt myself being pushed and I fell forward, out of the lorry's path as it missed me by inches. Someone had pushed me. It was Angela. She had been looking for me and she saw me, saw what I was doing – she risked her own safety to save me. I had been crying out for so long for someone, anyone, to help me, and I had carried on, always getting by on my own, fighting all the battles through all the years. But the work situation had been that final straw. I'd felt broken before, but now I really was.

There didn't seem any way forward from this awful state I was in, but, with the help and support of my family and close friends, I eventually found the strength to fight back in the only way I could. I took my case to a tribunal. In court, the statements from those who had plagued me, and driven me to try to take my own life, were so full of lies, I couldn't believe history was repeating itself again. They said I was a stripper and a pole dancer... if only I could be that agile – I can't climb a ladder, never mind a pole! They said I was a lesbian... one manager who had previously lived over the road from me stated that he had to move home because of me. I produced a copy of the repossession notice on his house and a copy of his bankruptcy notice, but no-one was interested. I was the only one telling the truth again, and I told how these people would pass remarks about me to each other in the office, I told how one of them had said *"Don't you think that women who've been abused turn to be lesbians?"* There were no limits to the cruelty of these people, and it is this kind of uneducated small-mindedness that builds the wall behind which abused people feel they need to hide.

The tribunal hearing lasted five days in all. One day, I turned up and I became so upset at having to listen to it all again, all the lies, all the ridiculous accusations, that I broke down completely. I realised I wasn't strong enough, at that time, to fight anything or anyone, and I decided this job was only causing me heartache and so it really wasn't worth fighting for.

It was at this point in time when Mom fell and

broke her hip, and I knew I had to rise above all of the rubbish, pull myself up and concentrate on caring for my mom.

This turning point in my life opened up a possibility that meant I could finally fulfil a dream that I'd carried with me for ages. Giving up work to be Mom's carer meant I would have the time and the opportunity to take a course in counselling, and I could train to be a real counsellor! Life was giving me the chance to work towards the one thing I always wanted to do.

Starting off on this new path made me realise I was ready to explore my own feelings, and so I arranged to have some counselling sessions. My counsellor was a lovely lady called Maureen, and she really helped me to move on in my life, to deal with the past and to put it firmly where it belonged – behind me.

One of the methods to help me achieve this was to write letters to 'my abuser' and 'my rapist'. I wrote one letter to each of them, telling them how I felt, explaining that, as long as I knew what they had done, so they would always know it, and I told them they were the ones living with the guilt, not me. Those letters were most significant for me, they created a real turning point, they allowed me to draw a line under the things I had been carrying with me for way too long, and now I could release those things, let them all go. All of the thoughts I'd kept in my head over the years, all the things I would say to my abusers... I didn't need to keep hold of them any longer. I could now say everything I wanted to, in writing, and, once I'd written it down, I posted the letters. It was an ending.

Chapter thirteen

The dogs' tale

Another change that marked this turning point in my life, this new beginning, was that I wanted to get a pet dog, which Eric didn't think was a good idea – but when did that ever stop me doing anything? Poor Eric had been very upset when the two dogs we'd had some time ago had to be put to sleep because of illness, and he really didn't want to have to go through that again with another dog. Of course, Eric saying no to me was completely the wrong answer!

I saw an advert for a dog rescue centre in Kidderminster and off I went to have a look, just to see what sort of dogs they had, and to find out what you had to do to adopt one. As I was wandering around the pens, all of the dogs were inside their kennels but there was this one female Staffy who was on top of her kennel, all wrapped up in a duvet, with just her eyes and nose showing. She looked a bit like ET!

I instantly knew she was different and I arranged to go back to collect her, after the people from the rescue centre had been to our house to do a home visit. They told me she wasn't very good at sharing things – toys, food and so on – and so she would sometimes snatch something from you. I saw this as a challenge and wasn't bothered at all, and very soon she was part of our family.

She tried to be the boss in the house but this was *my* home and I wouldn't let her. It was a proper battle of wills for a while, but then we grew on each other and, the more relaxed she became with me, so did I with her. I think I was just as good for her as she was for me, and I had found another friend — my friend, Bonnie. She's a real character and has some funny little habits: the odd way she sleeps and how she is cheeky and pushes you off the bench if you sit next to her, and the way she creeps into the house when you're not looking then hides out of your way. She is so entertaining, and so good to have around. A few years after Bonnie moved in, my friend Paul told me he had another Staffy needing to be re-homed, so I arranged to have this new addition to our household on a purely temporary basis until Diane was to take him to a woman she knew who wanted him. His name is Blade. Harry asked me if we could keep him and I said no because a lady was having him and she had children who were looking forward to having their own dog. I explained to Harry that we couldn't be selfish because we already had our Bonnie.

Meanwhile, Blade was getting more and more attached to us, I'm starting to feel sad for Harry having to let the dog go, then Diane told me the lady lived in a flat and she did have a dog but she gave it away because it was making a noise!

That was it. I wasn't going to let this lovely creature go to be stuck in a flat, being told to keep quiet all the time. It was me and Rex all over again – him in chains and me keeping quiet. So, Blade stayed. Bonnie accepted him because he accepted that she was the boss. Eric says I taught her well!

And so, what began as Eric not wanting one dog ended up with me getting two dogs! If I had the space, I'd have a houseful of dogs to care for, and Eric knows that, only too well. He'd say no, then he would let me do whatever I wanted to do anyway. It's one of the reasons I love him.

Chapter fourteen

Mom moving in

It was 2008 when I first enrolled for the Counselling course. Strangely, halfway through the course, our lecturer left and we had our fees reimbursed. It turned out to be Fate intervening, because, looking back, it wasn't the right time for me – I hadn't really *dealt with* my past, I'd simply locked it all away somewhere dark and quiet at the very back of my memory store, and that meant it would suddenly appear and confront me, at those times when I least expected it.

I had been immensely excited at the prospect of the course, and it was certainly the most challenging thing I had ever taken on. Before that, my life had consisted of looking after my eldest sister's kids, helping Mom with the housework, generally running around after all and sundry, and later – when Eric and I were married – it was all about setting up a nice home for us, a home that we worked very hard for. While I was working in the bookie's, Eric was working full-time in a local factory.

In 2009 when Mom had the bad fall and broke her hip, I couldn't let her go back to her filthy house, where my brothers and sisters would only visit to see what money they could get from her. It's hard to imagine, but my sister Brenda and brother Nigel would sometimes do the hoovering, wash the pots and do a bit of cleaning for Mom – and she would pay them! Brenda would borrow from Mom *'until I get my dole money'*, pay it back and then promptly borrow it back again. It was as if the money was on a length of elastic!

Nigel was even worse than that. Back in the 1980's, when Mom first had her hip replacement operation, we all visited her in hospital. When it was time to leave, Nigel said he had forgotten to give her a kiss and ran back to her ward: I followed him and walked in on him trying to bully Mom into giving him some money. Luckily, Dad had had the foresight to take her purse home with him. Dad knew what they were like with money, and he saw what a pushover Mom was with them. Nigel would tell Mom he needed the money for electric, gas and other bills, but it was really for ciggies and beer for him and his partner. He never paid Mom back.

Dad was diagnosed with cancer in 1998. One day, while walking me home, he confided in me that Craig had asked if Dad would lend him the cash to set up in business. I felt he was asking my advice, and I said, *"Well, you always taught us to stand on our own two feet, you've never given us money and we're your own kids. Craig is only our nephew."* I asked him what would Mom do for money if the debt wasn't paid back and Dad wasn't around to sort it out.

When Dad had been given twelve weeks to live, Craig tried again, asking for the money for a business. This is so callous, it's unbelievable.

Everyone would visit Mom when she was at her own house and they would make a real mess of the place – and not once bother to clean up. I would go round and clean the place from top to bottom, but, as soon as any of them turned up again, it would be just as bad, so I stopped doing it. I decided the best place for Mom was with us.

We were supposed to have a home assessment visit by Social Care, but no-one turned up for the appointment. I collected Mom from the hospital and it was a real struggle – with me, Diane, Shaun and his partner, Wayne – to manage getting her out of the car into a wheelchair, carry the wheelchair up the step into the porch and then somehow into the house and get her seated in a high-backed chair I'd bought specially. Mom had a problem with the chair when she was trying to lower herself into it or raise herself up out of it, and I approached Social Care and Inclusion for some assistance with this problem. I was told there was no funding available so I had no choice but to buy an electric recliner/riser chair, otherwise there was every chance Mom would have put too much strain on her new hip and on her heart. We also had problems getting Mom in and out of bed and I was having to drag her around her shoulders to lift her up, which was taking its toll on my back. Again, I asked for help but there was none.

I'd already had a shower cubicle installed for when Mom used to come and stay previously, but, with her new hip, she couldn't step into that. Until we could afford to pay a builder to strip the bathroom and turn it into a proper wet room, I had to sit Mom on the toilet and wash her with the shower hose. How undignified, and distressing for her. It's disgusting that people are having to 'make do' like this with aspects of daily life that are so important and so personal. We had to buy a rising toilet seat and grab rails to fit at either side, because there was no way Mom could use the toilet without these.

The only way I could get Mom out of the house to attend any medical appointments at the doctor's or the hospital, was with the help of three other people, so most of the time Mom and I were stuck in the house like prisoners. Luckily, Wayne managed to adapt a ramp for the front door, so I could manage the wheelchair better. The one medical aid we had been provided with – and even that was only on loan – was a walking frame, but it was on wheels and it would roll away from Mom when she tried to put her weight on it, so I ended up buying a better one. And so we got Mom settled in at our house. The money 'borrowing' had carried on after Dad died, but I didn't want to interfere because this was the first time Mom could make her own decisions, as Dad had always 'ruled' her. It took a lot for me to keep quiet, as I could see clearly that the others were just using her and really taking advantage.

Not long after she moved in with us, Mom told me Brenda had been asking to borrow 'a tenner', and she asked me what she should do. Nigel had just phoned and asked for money as well, 'for some bacca'... my response was to tell her, *"It's your money"*. I watched this go on for some months and kept wondering what they would do if Mom wasn't there to keep bailing them out; I didn't want to upset her and I wanted her to feel at home, I wanted to take care of her now and make the most of the years she had left.

One day, just after Brenda had left, Mom said she had asked for money again, and Mom told her she'd left her purse in the kitchen, which is where I was at the time. This was just the sign I needed to allow me to put a stop to this – if she was telling fibs about her purse, she really did want things to change. Mom told me she was sick of them coming round for money all the time, so I did what I had to do.

Next time each of them came 'to visit', I told them Mom wasn't going to be lending money any more, that she wasn't a bank, and I asked them what they thought they would do for money if Mom wasn't there. It was no shock to me when the visits all tailed off and eventually stopped altogether. Now, the only ones who come to see Mom and us are Diane, Sean Wayne and Shaun – out of a total of nine remaining siblings!

With only Eric working at the time, things were really difficult financially, especially with these extra costs, and this is how things remained until 2011 when a lovely District Nurse called Judith battled on our behalf and eventually got us an electric bed for Mom that would lift her up without assistance. Judith also arranged for us to have a proper ramp fitted – and, for her efforts, she was in real trouble with her managers for authorising these things. On her last visit, I thanked her with an arrangement of fresh flowers because I was so grateful. She had been the only person in the social care system who had actually listened to us.

We used up all of our savings on the adjustments to our home to accommodate Mom, which illustrates a sorry state of affairs for carers in the community who are saving the government millions of pounds. However wrong this is, and however angry it makes me, I would gladly do it all again because it meant being able to give Mom a better quality of life.

Chapter fifteen

Fulfilling my ambition

Another opportunity to take the counselling course presented itself in November 2010, and I enrolled at Wolverhampton College's Wellington Road Campus. My course tutor, Patty Jelic, appeared as a breath of fresh air for me because she put me at ease right from the first moment and I felt instantly relaxed with her. Thanks to her for the time, energy and commitment she gave to instill in me the basics to prepare me for the role of counsellor, and also to encourage my own personal growth.

Having *empathy* for others was easy for me because, as a survivor myself, I never wanted people to sympathise with me – I just wanted them to have some understanding of my past and how it had affected me.

The quality of *congruence* – being true to yourself, being a real and genuine person – I also found easy because I've never seen myself as either above or below other people, but always dealt with everyone on an equal footing. I've only ever wanted to have genuine people in my life and have always been interested in people as the individual he or she is. I've often been told throughout my life that I'm an easy person to talk to, and I've been described as open and honest without being brutal. My motto in life is, never look down on anyone because you never know when you might meet them again on your way down!

Unconditional Positive Regard, referred to as UPR, is the acceptance of people, however they appear – be that loving, proud, courageous, angry, fearful and so on. Again, because I accept all people in exactly the same way, and I believe we are all equal and all have the right to express ourselves, I can adjust to different life situations without passing judgement.

In a counselling environment, these three qualities make up the Core Conditions, so I felt I was halfway to being a good counsellor in my Level 1 course.

Then came *Active Listening*. I can listen to people all day long, but to be able to sit back and let someone speak without wanting to offer any help, feedback, suggestions… without wanting to get involved in a full-blown two-way conversation – I knew this was something I would struggle with. I've always enjoyed helping others with whatever problems or worries they had, but to simply listen and allow the other person to think for themselves without any input from me, was initially difficult for me. Finally, it sank in that letting the other person think for themselves is very important in leading them to make their own decisions, their own judgements, and to bring them back to a place where they can regain control of their own life.

It was strange because I now had children of my own and I was doing my best to bring them up to express themselves, to know they had choices and to have a voice so they could speak up for themselves and be heard. I realised I was growing with my children and that I needed to know they would be able to protect themselves if ever they needed to. I wanted to know they would speak out, shout and keep on shouting, until someone listened.

Moving on to Level 2 of the course with the amazing Patty as my tutor again, counselling was beginning to make more sense. I found I was starting to put these things into practice in my own life, instead of being held back by fear. I no longer needed to be afraid of what the family would think about me if I spoke my mind, if I told them what I really thought of them. I didn't have to worry about what they would do if I tried to disown them.

When I was young, my family would take an instant dislike to any friend I had, and they would constantly tell me how bad this person was for me, until I believed it myself. Looking back, I realise this was because they didn't want me getting close to someone so that I might confide in them about the abuse, might let them into our family secrets and this would mean the family would be shamed. Because of this 'overpowering' me all the time and running my life for me, I've always ignored what the family said and did to me. It was never spoken of, but I think they always sensed that I was somehow 'different' from the rest of them – I certainly knew it. I'm not ashamed of who I am and where I've come from, and I certainly have no skeletons in my own cupboard.

The best thing is that, now I have Eric and the boys – a real family – I'm not at all worried about upsetting my birth family because I no longer want to be a part of them, and I don't need to be accepted by them.

I have my own family, my own identity. For once in my life, I'm in a very, very good place.

Chapter sixteen

Coping with the bad times

Charlie's accident

Towards the end of 2012, we had a particularly busy time when Mom had been ill, both Shaun and Wayne were very ill after both suffering a stroke, and Shaun had a nervous breakdown at the same time, so, as a family, we were all over the place. Harry went to stay with Shaun and Wayne to help them and Charlie was helping at home with his nan. A friend decided we could do with a bit of a treat and, as it was almost Bonfire Night, she organised a firework party. I sent Eric and the boys off to spend some relaxing time together while I went to help Shaun and Wayne and my sister-in-law, Viv, looked after Mom for me. My mobile rang and it was Diane saying Charlie had had an accident but I wasn't to worry and she had taken him and Eric to Walsall Manor hospital. She promised to call me again as soon as she had news. I didn't really worry, because Charlie was with his dad, so I knew he was safe. Then, I had another call telling me Charlie had to go to the eye infirmary at New Cross hospital and asking me if I could meet them there. I felt sick.

I hurried to the hospital and met up with the others. Charlie had a nasty eye injury caused by a firework going astray and hitting him in his left eye. Eric was in a bad way, blaming himself for what had happened, but my attitude is that these things are just part of destiny, life's rich pattern, being in the wrong place at the wrong time.

I took Charlie in to see the doctor and he seemed quite positive, giving us some eye drops and asking us to go back at eleven o'clock the next morning. We were really shocked to receive a phone call at seven a.m. from the consultant, asking us to go in as soon as we could, which we did. We really weren't prepared for what came next – the doctor told us Charlie had lost the sight in his left eye and that this was going to be permanent. Charlie and I both cried at hearing this, and we went home to tell Eric. He was heartbroken, and feeling terribly guilty, even though it was really no-one's fault.

This left us on something of a roller coaster, having been told that Charlie might have to lose his eye completely because the retina had become detached, then Charlie had an emergency operation around Christmas time. After that, he suffered with double vision constantly... it was all dreadful, and so sad.

We were desperate to know how this would affect Charlie's chances of taking on medical training, because he'd always wanted, with all his heart, to be a doctor. And would he be able to drive a car? How would the injury affect different aspects of his life, his future? Was there something, anything, that could be done to help him? We needed to know that Charlie could go on to do the things he wanted to do and to live a full and happy life.

Since then, against all the odds, Charlie passed his driving test at the first attempt – what an achievement! Of course, his studies have been affected but he's working very hard to catch up again. Charlie has faced these hurdles head-on, and he's managed to overcome them through his own resilience and strength of character, and with our support and our love. Eric still beats himself up but me and Charlie just agree with him when he says it was all his fault, because we know this will make him fight back, which is far better than keeping it all shut away inside where it would just make him ill again.

For me, I was upset because I couldn't stand to see Charlie's life turned upside down, to see him not be able to live as he wanted to.

On Tuesday, the eighth of October, 2012, a Harley Street consultant came to see us at home to make a diagnosis of the condition of Charlie's eye. This followed a claim we made against the firework manufacturer. Charlie told the doctor he would sooner not have had the accident and kept his sight, rather than be fighting for justice now. The doctor confirmed that the injury was a serious one – a chorioretinal rupture – and that he would class Charlie's left eye as a blind eye, adding that there was no cure for it at present. He did mention that, within the next five to ten years, there could well be a procedure to rectify the damage. He gave his advice regarding Charlie's hopes of working in medicine, saying he should consider becoming a clinical scientist by going into bio-medicine studies, then he could go on to gain a degree in medicine.

I wished I could take the pain, the injury, instead of Charlie, but life's not like that and I know that he will be all the stronger for this awful thing that happened. The one thing it did for me was to allow me to worry less about the boys' safety all the time, to stop 'smothering' them, maybe… and just be their mother instead.

Eric's heart attack

In July, 2013, Eric started having headaches, really terrible ones that he couldn't get rid of, so he went to the doctor. His blood pressure was too high and he was sent home with a twenty-four-hour monitor, then back to the surgery the next day, when the nurse gave him an ECG. She wasn't happy with the results of this test and said she thought there might be a slight rhythm imbalance, so Eric was to go back again the following week. I went with him for this appointment.

The doctor sat us both down and said, *"Has anyone told you anything?"* and we said not really, so he carried on, *"Well, I don't want you to worry, but it looks like you've had a heart attack. We can't tell when this happened and you need to go to hospital right away."* Eric was, understandably, very upset at hearing this – it had come as such a shock. I rang Sean Wayne to ask him to go and sit with Mom and the boys at our house, but told him to make sure he didn't mention anything because I didn't want Mom to get upset or worried.

I took Eric to New Cross Hospital in Wolverhampton and they decided to admit him for tests. He was allowed to go home later the same day and all he'd been told was *"There isn't much we can do because you've had a heart attack but we don't know when."* Back at the house, I carried on as normal, trying not to let Eric or Mom see just how concerned I was, but Eric couldn't hide his own feelings. I knew he was very worried, as anyone would be. Over the weekend, he began to have chest pains so I took him to Walsall Manor Hospital, where he was kept in for a few days and had all sorts of tests – scans, blood tests, an angiogram... everything they could do in the circumstances. The staff there were very good and helpful, but still there was no real answer. Eric was sent home and told to rest, and he had some medication to take.

This has been a real roller-coaster for us – never really knowing what was happening, whether it was actually a heart attack or not, being told, *"Yes, he has had a heart attack"*, then *"No, it wasn't a heart attack"*, and *"Yes, it was a heart attack but we don't know when it happened so we can't do anything."* I'm very much a person who gets on with life, but the thought that I might lose Eric was too dreadful and I was terrified: I couldn't bear to think the boys might have to be without their dad. They idolise him. When they play fight with him and he wants them to stop, he'll say, *"Oh, no! stop! I can't breathe... my heart!"* but the boys don't buy it, and we just know he's being a crackpot.

As for me, I might not say it often enough but I love him to bits.

Chapter seventeen

My friends, my chosen family

Sameem

I worked for a while in a local betting shop owned by one of the large national bookmakers, as cleaner, cashier and also as manager. I loved my job at the 'bookie's' because the customers I was dealing with were all so different – some were just simple, happy souls who were content to place a couple of little bets and then go home in the same jovial frame of mind as when they'd arrived: at the other extreme were those who obviously had a bit of a problem with gambling and they would get very antagonistic towards the staff – almost as if we had taken their money forcibly!

Through this interchange with all of these characters, I learned how to handle people in various situations – the nice ones and the not-so-nice ones. It was a challenge and I was proud of myself when I realised I was able to calm the irate customers down, and even gain their respect. This would be reflected whenever I bumped into them around the town and they would actually stop to chat with me. I found this incredibly rewarding and it gave me the idea that I really did have some of the skills to build on, such as being non-judgemental and empathetic, and this could set me on the road to becoming a counsellor.

When I look back, I see I was using these natural skills while I was growing up and the abuse was going on: I wouldn't let what was happening to me tarnish my views of other people, and I was able to feel empathy towards friends who were going through their own ordeals, whatever those were. One particular friend who went to the same school as me, a lovely girl called Sameem, confided in me that her Pakistani family were abusing her. They treated her like a slave, making her do all the work around the house, wait on them hand and foot, and they beat her badly on a regular basis.

Sameem was a tall, slender girl with eyes so big and dark, but there was no light in those eyes, no life shining through. Her long black hair was always greasy and smelled of engine oil, and she walked with a sort of shuffle, as if she was afraid to move. She had awful bruising all over her body and it was clear that she was being mistreated. She was terrified and distraught. The poor girl had a speech impediment and would stammer quite badly most of the time — this was, of course, made worse by her fear and stress — and this made it very difficult for her to talk about her situation. She was in floods of tears, shaking violently, and she told me she simply couldn't go on. She said she wanted to die.

Sameem was a true friend to me and a beautiful soul. She certainly didn't deserve the life she was forced to live. My heart went out to her and I knew I had to do whatever I could to help her. I encouraged her to speak to a teacher, as I knew they would have to deal with the matter properly and she would get the help and support she so badly needed. Unfortunately, our next lesson was to be with a teacher who was Pakistani, and Sameem insisted she couldn't tell anyone of her own race because the first thing they would do was report it to her family's community, and this would lead to even more beatings — possibly worse. I tried to reassure her, and we agreed that, once this lesson was over, we would go to the headmaster's office and I would stay with her while she told her dreadful story. Once inside the Head's study, Sameem started stammering uncontrollably and sobbing, so I began to speak on her behalf, telling the Head what she had told me. He listened to what I was saying, but he needed to ask her questions to make certain she was telling the truth, then he said he needed to make a phone call, at which point I was ushered out of the room as he told me hurriedly that I *must not* speak of this to anyone. I knew, all too well, what it meant when an adult told a child they mustn't speak about things… I felt I had helped my friend to open up about her own situation, and I thought that, if it worked out well for her after this disclosure, then I would be able to tell of my own abuse.

Not long after this meeting, Sameem disappeared from the school and, no matter who I asked, no-one could (or would?) tell me anything – in fact, I got the feeling they didn't even care what had happened to her. I just hoped she was in a better place, somewhere safe, but – for my own part – without her beside me, there was no chance of me telling my own story.

When I lost my friend, Sameem, I lost my courage and my resolve. Anyway, my brothers, sisters and cousins all went to the same school, so there was every chance Derek would hear about it if I did tell, and I didn't dare consider what might happen then.

I never knew what happened to Sameem. As the years passed by, I often thought about her and wondered how life was treating her. More recently, I started reading true life story books, as I was considering writing my own book, and – purely by accident – I found a book entitled *'Belonging'*, written by my old friend, Sameem. In it, she tells her harrowing story, from life in an orphanage, through the abuse at the hands of her own family, a forced marriage at the age of thirteen and having a baby shortly after that... I learned from the book that she eventually ran away, escaped from her dreadful existence, with her child.

As I read through those pages, I realised why I wanted to write my own book. Like Sameem, I want other kids who are suffering in silence to avoid being ignored, being abandoned by the system, I want them to have their own voice. Kids are resilient – up to a point, but there has to be a limit to this. Society and the so-called child protection that is in place should be held responsible when yet another child's appalling story hits the headlines *because no-one listened.*

Lisa

Having my family around me is a blessing I can't put into words, and I'm even more blessed because the true friends I've made, who will be my friends forever – whatever – are my 'extended family'. At least, that's how I see them.

I met Lisa at the children's school in 2001 through a mutual friend. She had given birth to her son, Adam, in May that year and in the December I had Harry. One day, after delivering the kids to school, Lisa was heading off to town and I had my car so I offered her a lift. A very simple beginning to what became a very solid friendship.

At first, we'd just chit-chat, pass the time of day, but we soon realised we could tell each other anything without pretence, without hesitation and without either of us ever taking offence. Our conversations flowed so easily and we could laugh together – real laughter from our bellies, laughter with eyes watering and noses snorting. No-limits laughter.

Our friendship is based on one thing – honesty. Lisa is real, her family mean everything to her and she would do anything for her children: this is the quality that first drew me to her. Lisa is down-to-earth, what you see is definitely what you get, and she is most excellent at having fun. We've shared some really silly times together, finding humour in anything and everything. More often than not, we didn't need anything to *be* funny, to set us off. Once, we were in my car driving through town, taking Charlie to a concert where he was singing with the choir. We were teasing him about his backing singers, and we turned up the car radio and started singing – or maybe screeching is a better word – at the tops of our voices, along with whatever song was trying to come out of the speakers. We were in the middle of town and the car windows were down – Charlie, bless him, was not amused, but we were roaring with laughter.

Lisa and the laughter helped me regain some of the life I'd lost as a child. The laughter, the trust and the sense of belonging.

There was an awful incident at the primary school when Charlie was being severely bullied and a teacher had told him *"You don't have to tell your mommy everything"*. I was fuming. I'd always taught my boys to speak up and not to keep any secrets, and this teacher – who should have been teaching the same principles – was trying to overturn what I was doing my best to achieve.

Lisa's daughter had seen Harry being hit during the school break and she spoke to the teacher, who told her she couldn't possibly have seen anything like that, even though the little girl was very insistent. Lisa confronted the headmistress about her daughter being called a liar, and then she went to have it out with the bully's parents. This is when the headmistress told Lisa she should really keep away from me, otherwise she'd be 'tarred with the same brush'. So, Lisa was the one doing the fighting, but I got the blame! We laugh about it to this day.

Lisa was there for me when my Harry was very ill and had lots of hospital visits because of his asthma; she was there when I lost my brother, Ronnie, to cancer; there when I had a breakdown, when Mom became ill… and I've been there for her when she lost her dad, her nan and her granddad, all to cancer and all in a very short space of time.

I love everything about Lisa and her family, and they will always be part of me and my family. She's my *chosen* sister.

Angela

Angela was a little girl whose family lived along the street from Pat and Steve's, and Hayley used to play with her sister, Nichola. I knew her mom and dad to speak to and they were always very pleasant. One day, Nichola came across to Pat's to ask if she could use the phone to ring for an ambulance because Angela had had a seizure. She was epileptic. I didn't really see much of her while I was growing up, but years later when I had my second son, Harry, Angela's baby boy was born not long after that, and we started to build a friendship, helping each other out with little odd jobs to ease the strain of being mums with new babies. Eric and I had just moved into our house in Dryden Road with Charlie and now baby Harry as well, and Angela was still living in Keats Road. When we had moved to Stanley Street towards the end of 2003, she appeared again a year or so later, coming to live just round the corner from us. Fate seemed to be putting us into each other's lives.

I started going round to her place but I really wasn't keen on her partner because he was very controlling and he told terrible lies – my two pet hates in people. He reminded me of his dad, who I'd known from years ago (his dad and I were from the same era, whereas Angela was about thirteen years younger than me). His dad was controlling and violent towards his children. He was often at the local bingo evenings with his mother, while his wife was suffering with cancer and was dying at home. Their neighbours would help out when she became really poorly because the dad did nothing to take care of the poor woman. When Angela's ex was a young lad, he had to do the washing, the cooking, the cleaning, and he looked after his younger sister. Their dad didn't care about his children, only the money that came from having them. When their mom passed away, the daughters didn't lift a finger to help with anything – no doubt because they had seen the way their dad had treated Mom.

The dad was always in the bookie's where I worked, gambling and losing money, which obviously didn't help his temper, and I know he used to throw the furniture about when he'd lost again. Once, when he was walking past our house in Dryden Road and the children were following behind him, he suddenly swung round on them, punching the boy hard between the shoulder blades, making his little body lurch forward, and he smacked the girl in the mouth. This was nothing but abuse, and Eric ran out into the street, shouting to their dad to leave them alone. Eric was fuming, and he confronted their dad with *"How would you like a smack from me?"* I had to drag Eric back to the house, he was so angry. We both hate child abuse and that's exactly what this was – no wonder Angela's ex followed in his dad's footsteps. He was friendly with Hayley and my sister, Pat – until he stole her purse when he was visiting her one time.

This is the opposite side of the 'learned behaviour' coin from my own story. Whereas I removed myself from everything my family had stood for, Angela's ex was trapped into becoming just the same as his role model.

My visits to Angela's weren't very frequent but we always invited each other's kids to any birthday parties, so we kept the friendship going. Then she and her partner decided to get married, and Lisa and I were helping Angela look for her dress for the wedding. While the three of us were going round the shops, she suddenly opened up to us, saying she didn't want to marry this chap but she was scared of him and felt she couldn't get out of it. She really confided in us and we could see, without a doubt, how unhappy she was – plus, he was threatening her. All I could do was advise her that she mustn't worry about other people, about letting anyone down, and she shouldn't fret about what people would say. I told her it was her happiness that mattered, nothing else.

The wedding went ahead and she made a very reluctant bride, marrying out of the fear of what others would think of her, as well as fear of her new husband. The marriage didn't work out, going rapidly downhill through domestic violence and him having an affair with another man, who he later moved in with.

Angela had developed pre-cancerous colitis, and

he would use this, as well as her epilepsy, to threaten her and keep her completely under his control. He would tell her the children would be taken into care because of her health problems. Towards the end of their relationship, she was confined to bed quite a lot of the time because he was administering her medication, overdosing her so people would see her as a real invalid and he would be seen as the caring one! An effect of the extra medication was to make her appear 'drunk' and he told her nobody would believe anything she said because they would say it was just the drink. He would hide her bank cards on top of the kitchen cupboards and, whenever Angela eventually found them, he'd blame their son, telling the poor boy to say sorry and *"Tell your Mommy you hid her card!"*, which was mental cruelty. He hit the boy for wetting the bed, on one occasion head-butting him and breaking his nose. He bought a car that he shouldn't have been driving because he didn't have a licence, and sneaked the kids out in it while Angela was in hospital, risking their lives because he was both an illegal driver and an inexperienced one. When her brother died and she was at her dad's house, helping get the house ready for the funeral, he rang to tell her the fridge door had fallen off and he needed her to come home right away. She told him she'd be there as soon as she could, so he stamped all over the door, damaging it even more. His son had seen him dismantle the door – this was just more tantrum throwing, more attempting to control. Just like his dad.

He even tried to move his 'friend' into their home, a chap who Angela later discovered was her husband's boyfriend! There was nothing he wouldn't stoop to. What with the verbal abuse, the threats, the physical violence, all constant and with no relief, Angela was eventually beaten down, to the point where she had no self-esteem, no strength and absolutely no thought for herself. She felt she was worthless. He controlled her with his lies and she believed every word.

Even after they split up, he still controlled her. She let him come to her house every day for meals and to stay involved with the 'family life' – such as it was. The only thing he didn't do was sleep there, but nothing else had really changed.

In 2009, my son Charlie set up a Facebook account for me, thinking it would help me with my counselling studies, but it didn't really interest me and I didn't use it. Out of the blue, I started receiving messages from Angela's ex – to begin with, I ignored them but my mobile phone was linked to my email account and soon I was getting messages from him at all hours of the day and night. Before long, the messages were abusive. I had to get Charlie to help me send him a message, telling him I didn't want to know, and that what he was doing was wrong. The messages carried on coming through and soon I'd had enough of it so I went to see Angela and asked her to tell him, next time she saw him, that I didn't want to be involved and that he must stop sending me any messages. Of course, he wouldn't give up and he started sending messages that were even worse, calling me a slag, bitch, lesbian, whore – all of which I found funny. One day I was at Angela's, having a coffee and a chat, when he brought the kids back, so I went outside to speak to him. I told him to leave me out of his fights and his gossip, I told him I just wasn't interested. All he did was make things worse. He got back in his car and started shouting at me – abuse, threats, anything he could think of. That didn't bother me, until he said *"Pat and Hayley said you was a nutter 'cos you was raped by your brother!"*

That knocked me for six. How could people be so evil? Until then, I hadn't realised how manipulative he could be – and there was more to come. Angela's kids were still visiting their dad and one day the daughter told me her dad was getting someone to beat me up, she said he told her I was a scrubber, a lesbian… I listened to what she had to say and then I just said *"He's silly, take no notice, it doesn't matter,"* but, inside, I was screaming. Why would he want to put such things in the heads of his little children, using them like that, confusing them? Why?

I cancelled my Facebook account, and I realised why Jeremy Kyle, in his TV show, was always telling everyone not to use it. With this loss of contact, Angela's ex realised he was losing control of her and he retaliated, trying to poison her against me. This didn't work, so he started playing with her mind. He'd send the kids back from a visit, having told them to trash their room at home, to kick their mom so that she'd have a fit, to tell Mom they were going to have to live with Dad... why couldn't he just go away and get on with his own life?

The children were telling about his abusive treatment of them and so Angela stopped him seeing them altogether. He then began sitting outside their house, like some mad stalker, frightening the children so they didn't want to go home, so I would have them to stay with us for a while. He would wait for the house to be empty, then he'd let himself in and let their dog loose into the street, to roam around by a busy main road. The kids loved their dog, and, luckily, neighbours caught the poor thing before it got run over. We had a padlock fitted to the gates after that. He came back again and moved some plant pots around in the garden – just to let Angela know he could come back at any time – and, when the plants were all in full bloom, he threw weed killer all over them.

It was after the children disclosed to counsellors what was going on that Angela asked to be moved to a safe house: she didn't want to leave her home but the safety and wellbeing of her children had to come first. We were constantly going to the police station to report him, but they weren't very helpful: all they said was, they couldn't get involved unless he harmed her or the children. Isn't that a bit too late? Why should she or her children become yet another statistic?

When I started my counselling course, I couldn't leave Mom on her own so I asked Diane and Brenda to help out. Diane would come and get Mom out of bed, showered and dressed, then Brenda was to take over when Diane went to work. Diane did her bit but Brenda, true to form, never turned up so Angela took care of Mom during the day. Angela has always been there for me, and I know I can trust her, one hundred per cent, to look after Mom properly. One day while she was covering for me with Mom, she had to ring for an ambulance because Mom had developed pneumonia and she was in a bad way. Brenda appeared at the hospital and tried to push Angela out of the way, but Diane stopped her. How dare she do that to my friend, who was helping out, when she herself hadn't even bothered to turn up, and was completely avoiding any responsibility towards our ailing Mom?

Angela is a *good* person who has had a raw deal in life. She lost her mom and her brother, and now her dad has been diagnosed with cancer. She really could do with a break. But, against all the odds, Angela has raised three lovely children, all beautiful natured, and I love them as if they were my own. Angela and I have a sort of mother-daughter relationship, because I like to take care of her as she deserves. She can be stubborn and independent, just like me! – which is probably why we get on so well. Like Lisa, Angela is here for life, and if I could scoop us all up and move us away together, I would do it tomorrow. As opposed to the 'family' I was born into, Angela is my sister of choice.

Paul

I first met Paul when I started my job as a parking warden. He had been doing the job for a while and he made me feel very welcome, helping me to settle in and, when I was doing my training, he was my partner. Quite a tall man with a solid build, silver haired and absolutely crackers, Paul introduced himself as *"the only gay in here because there's no room for any more,"* using his humour as an icebreaker to let me know about his sexuality right from the start, which I appreciated. It certainly didn't shock me, seeing as I have a brother who is gay, and it would never be a problem for me.

When we were working together, Paul would have me in fits of laughter and people would come up to us and say what a pleasure it was to see happy traffic wardens because most of the ones they saw were miserable. We shared the same belief that, if you talk to people with respect and explain to them what they are doing wrong – in this case, they were parking incorrectly – there was much more chance that they would listen and take on board what you were saying, and they would try to avoid the same situation in future.

Just slapping parking tickets on people's cars and disappearing without a word doesn't really help the problem. Dealing with people in this way meant they would overlook the uniform and they would listen to us.

> By simply being friendly and helpful, rather than being aggressive and alienating people, we actually made friends among the public as we went about our duties. To this day, if Paul and I are out and about together, some people still remember us and they stop for a chat. I see this as quite an achievement, and it's how things should be.

Paul's joyful sense of humour was infectious. One Christmas, he and I opted to work the late shift and do the locking up so that the rest of the staff could go on the company Christmas night out to the dog racing. I'd had enough of dog racing and gambling when I worked for the bookies, and Paul wasn't a betting man, so neither of us really minded missing the event. During the evening, Paul confided in me that he had once been in a relationship with a woman and they had had children, before he owned up to being gay, Some time later, while Eric and I were chatting with Paul and another friend, Paul admitted he had been reeling us in again when he had told that story. We'd all believed it for ages and, when he said he was joking, we just fell about laughing.

Paul became a tremendous source of support

for me later in this employment when a colleague began a campaign against me to make me appear bad at my job. This person would hide my notes that I had written and would need again, they would hide other information such as details of forthcoming events and so on, they would lock barriers behind me and other childish things, all of which was making me look incompetent.

This behaviour caused me a lot of upset but Paul would talk me out of my distress and tell me to carry on with my head held high because I was the better person. I did try but this constant daily battle became too much to bear and I gave my notice in. We had a new office manager, and she persuaded me to stay on. I did stay for a while but, unbelievably, this manager teamed up with the person who had been bullying me and then I had the two of them to contend with. Paul was my shoulder to cry on and his silly banter was a great distraction. He always managed to turn me around and I would never cry for very long.

When Mom broke her hip and I took on caring for her, I finally left this job. While she was in hospital in a pretty bad way, Paul's mom, Pauline, was rushed in to the same unit and was put in a bed alongside Mom in the ward. Paul asked me if I would mind keeping an eye on her while I was there, because it was plain to see the nurses were all rushed off their feet and could do with some help. Because he had been so supportive to me and had become such a good friend, I was more than happy to repay his kindness by looking after Pauline and I became very close to her and Paul's family.

Paul's brother once asked him if I was pregnant. Unfortunately, I was suffering from stress-related IBS and one of the symptoms was a rather bloated tummy! When he came to visit the next time, I said to the brother *"How dare you say I'm pregnant – I'm just FAT!"* The poor chap's face turned crimson, while Paul and I were in hysterics.

Paul eventually paid the price for being my friend when he was told by the office manager at work that he must not talk to me. Of course, Paul carried on being friends with me because we both believe friendship is more important, and it was not the place of someone at work to tell anyone who they could or couldn't socialise with. This resulted in him being treated in much the same way as I'd had to put up with, and then he was given the sack, and this was used as an opportunity to verbally abuse him about his sexuality.

I was furious to hear this and I helped Paul as much as I could, standing as a witness to the treatment he'd received, which at least made the company pay him off properly. We celebrated this victory over abuse (and stupidity) with coffee and sandwiches. While we were eating, I picked up the sauce bottle and started shaking it, but the top flew off and the sauce splashed all over the walls, the floor – and me! We both fell into one of our fits of laughter and I was never sure if Paul had set me up that time.

Both our moms made their recovery and came home, and we all started visiting each other. I always feel so welcome at Paul's family home, and we never fail to have such a lot of fun and laughs. We go on shopping trips, take our moms to various functions, and there's never a dull moment in the time we spend together.

What I really love about Paul is that he can turn a bad day into a good one with his humour, and, in my new life, laughter is definitely the best medicine. Paul and his family will always be part of my new family – my true friends, my family of choice.

Chapter eighteen

Friends from learning and sharing

Sarah

While I was working through the first three levels of the counselling course, we each had a learning partner so we could help each other and have someone for support with our class work and the various assignments. My learning partner was Sarah.

Because of the horrid experiences I'd had at work before starting the course I was finding it hard to trust anyone and I would dislike people when I first met them and wait until they could prove themselves worthy of my trust. I'd find I was asking myself, wondering if someone was sincere or not, and not knowing whether I should make that decision, just in case they let me down. This was a difficult way to be, to live, because I was judging people and I'd never been like that in my whole life, so feeling like this was making me unhappy with myself.

Sarah's warmth and friendship, and her constant encouragement, helped me find myself again without even realising it.

When she left after Level 3, we kept in touch and carried on meeting up in town for a catch-up. I know we will always be friends and I'll always be grateful for her friendship and her support.

Danielle

When Sarah left the course, Danielle became my learning partner and with her I learned to develop another side to myself. Before this, I would always do things for others because I would feel selfish if I didn't help them, but Danielle taught me that not allowing others to do things was actually preventing them from growing as individuals.

Danielle appears outwardly quiet and reserved, but she has great inner strength and determination. She showed me I should not feel guilty when she wanted to do something for herself, and she gave me permission to stand back and observe. This meant I was now free of all the guilt I'd carried around with me for the whole of my life, the guilt that had been instilled in me by my birth family and their 'family values.' I no longer had to apologise or justify myself when I wasn't being helpful to someone.

Danielle helped me to realise *I could say no.*

Andrea

Andrea taught me a lot, without even knowing she was doing it, because she made me feel comfortable when I asked for her help – she always encouraged me to ask. She would offer her help and then she'd stand back and wait for me to ask. The more I got used to asking, the more comfortable it felt and I found I could ask someone who happened to be around for his or her help. I reached a point where I didn't feel insecure about my ability to do things for myself. My confidence in myself was developing, was being nurtured by kind words, kind gestures and genuine support.

I was being encouraged to grow to my full potential.

Ken

With Ken, I learned how to include fun in what we were doing – he always brought fun into the classroom and he loved playing the clown (the face behind the mask). With his black-and-white logic and his mischievous grin spread across his friendly face, he'd have me shaking my head at him from the other side of the room. Ken is kind, caring, and very intelligent, but he can behave in the most bonkers way at times, bringing us all into fits of laughter.

Ken has shown me that it's OK to have

alternative thinking because that's what makes us all unique in our own right. He knows me, just the same as I know him, and I can cry to him, laugh with him, ask for his help and tell him absolutely anything without feeling judged.

Ken taught me to trust myself, to trust others, to have fun and live life to the full. He is my 'away-from-home Eric' while I'm at college – and that's a huge compliment!

Chapter nineteen

Making a stand

I'd lived with fear constantly and it came in many guises. There was the fear of Derek and what he was doing to me, the fear of Dad finding out about it, the fear of having to do things I didn't want to do because I was being bullied and/or blackmailed by the threat of someone telling Dad my awful secret, the fear of what Dad would do to Mom if he found out because he would blame her for letting it happen…

There was that time when Diane had made me pull this girl's hair – I really didn't want to do it, but I was scared Diane would hit me if I didn't do what she said. When I went to live with Pat and Steve, I was too afraid to question anything they asked of me because I knew I'd be sent back home. Everything I did, everything I thought, and everything I was – it was all out of fear.

Once, in a fit of blinding anger and the

overwhelming desire to get my own back on Derek, I climbed over the fence into his garden and trashed all the marrows he'd been growing. Any sense of satisfaction I may have had was short-lived because then came the fear that maybe someone had seen me do it, maybe Dad would find out... my entire existence was built on fear – right up until I met Eric.

Since Mom moved in with us, I really started to feel enormous resentment towards my birth family, and I didn't want to be part of their dysfunctional tribe any longer. When they came to see Mom, I found myself listening to their stories, their secrets and lies – all the time swearing each other – and me – to secrecy because, heaven forbid, I should repeat any of their ridiculous outpourings to the others in the family.

I was sick of their nastiness, the lies and deceit they fed on, and I told them they were here, in my home, to see their mother and that, when her time of passing came, they would no longer be my family. One time when Sean Wayne was visiting, he was openly talking about Derek, saying he'd always known Derek was a 'kiddy fiddler' and such like. He was talking about this in such a matter-of-fact way, as if it was ordinary and mundane – and all in front of my two boys. That made me see red and a part of me wanted to scream out *"Yes! And that kiddy was me!"*

So much of what I was hearing proved to me

that I had been lied to such a lot over the years, and I realised what strange individuals these people were. Family they may be, but I hardly knew them. The more I heard, the more angry and upset I became: they were talking about things decent people wouldn't speak of in front of youngsters, and they even thought some of the things they were saying were funny. I was boiling over with anger.

My boys started passing comments back to me from these 'conversations', and telling me the others were asking them questions. I could see the beginnings of grooming and an attempt to take control, and I was *not* going to tolerate this. I told my sons not to listen to these lies, adding that they should feel free to answer back if they wanted to. I needed the boys to know these people were not the family they should follow or trust, and that they should use their own judgement of others. Just being part of the same family doesn't automatically assume loyalty.

I had reached a point in my life where, instead of always helping people, I was able to give others – in this case, my sons – the tools to help themselves, make their own decisions, live their own lives. I was enabling them. At first, this freedom I was giving them came as a shock, even with the smallest things, like making their own drinks or getting their own clothes, but it soon became a normal part of our family life.

My 'birth family', on the other hand, didn't

take to this because they wanted me to carry on doing things for them. I could now sit back and let them ask me to do something several times and not respond – only to be told I was selfish!

I realised that the counselling courses were doing this for me. I wasn't simply taking in the knowledge, but I was putting it into practice in my own life – I was making a stand against the tyranny of my family, and I wasn't feeling scared of being punished, or worried about being ignored.

I had promised myself that my boys would have a very different life to the one I'd had, but, most important of all, in our family there would be no lies. It's my pet hate in life, because, if you are telling a lie, you're protecting someone who is behind that lie.

When I had progressed to Level 3 of the counselling course, I had a new tutor, a lady called Caroline who was warm and friendly but, at the same time, I knew she would be the making of me. She was always firm but fair and pushed me to my limits, which I needed and wanted. Cal, as she preferred us to call her, was passionate about person-centred counselling and she lived and breathed it. At this level, our work focused a lot on criteria (this is about how learning outcomes to the question can be applied and this has to be shown in the written work) throughout our journals and assessments. We had to acknowledge that we could understand counselling – what it is and how it is applied. Even with my love of working with figures, dealing with criteria, which were all numbered, for example, 1.1, 1.2, 1.3 and so on, was very frustrating and I was seeing numbers in my sleep!

One aspect of the work at this stage that I really loved was the weekly journaling, because I was able to express myself completely openly and honestly as a person, as an individual – as me, DAWN. I hadn't kept a diary of any kind since we had lived in Keats Road and Diane had found that one and then she took a great deal of pleasure in teasing me with the things I'd written. She didn't find the other diary, the one I kept hidden under the floorboards. It was in those pages that I wrote down all of the horrible things Derek was doing to me.

After the humiliation of Diane's discovery, I decided it was too much of a risk to write things down, so I kept everything in my head, all stored in my memory, which was a bad thing because they could come out at any time and catch me by surprise, throw me right back to the time when it all happened. It's very helpful to be able to write about your troubles, your fears, your secrets, because it gets them out from the inside, it makes them external to you, the person, makes you feel somehow separate from them. I do believe not having this form of 'release' had been the beginning of my downward spiral.

I survived Level 3 and I passed! Now I was headed towards the Diploma, the next level. For this,

I was going to need to commit the time needed to devote to my studies, including one full day each week at college. There were going to be a lot of essays to write, a lot of research to be done, reading, personal therapy, supervision and a trainee placement to work through.

The placement part of the course is to undertake a number of hours of giving counselling to my own clients, for which I have to be accepted in a recognised professional centre. My first placement didn't materialise, purely because of the timescale, but I applied for another, had the interview and have been offered the placement. This is in bereavement support, so I'll be counselling people who have lost someone close to them. I've had the training, my criminal records check has been done, I'm having supervision sessions and am now waiting to see my first client.

I need to complete one hundred and fifty hours with clients before next July (2014), so I've taken another placement in a secondary school where I'll be working with young adults, once I've had the interview and the training at the Joseph Leckie Academy. It wasn't easy to find placements within the Walsall Borough but it's essential that I'm close to home for Mom and the boys.

I'm enjoying my course and I'm getting so much from it. Both Patty, my previous tutor, and Cal have given me such a lot of positive feedback, along with the encouragement to carry on. I did struggle for a while with the essays because I've always been more of a practical learner rather than an academic one. This course was a really huge undertaking for me.

As well as the things that have happened since I started the course, things that really tested my determination to stick with it – for example, Eric's heart attack, Charlie's eye accident, and so on – I have seen my friend's children let down, completely failed in the worst way, by the services that are supposed to be in place to protect them. These children went to social services and told of their dad beating their brother (he once broke the boy's nose by head-butting him) and how the little girl was made to pull her pants down so they could all look at her 'mini moo' and then humiliate the child by all laughing at her.

The police were called in and they interviewed the children, their dad and his family, and passed the case to the CPS but they wouldn't pursue it, even though all of the statements were different! They weren't all telling the same story, which says there was something wrong somewhere. But, once again, no-one saw this was an issue and no-one could be bothered to look into it any further. The dad was allowed to fight for access in court and the officer from the court support services didn't ask for reports from the children's school or from the counsellors the children had seen, and she told the children *"You will have to see your dad... I didn't see mine but then I made friends with him."* The judge who heard the case said he didn't know anything about child protection cases. It's so unbelievable.

These children have been brave enough to speak up and they have told all of these professionals what was going on, but they have been failed by the services because their father is allowed to see them again. They have been knocked back and will find it very difficult to trust or to speak out again if something else happens to them. That is, if they don't become just another statistic in the headline news when their father has killed them. Nothing seems to have changed in the forty years since I was a child in need of help.

WHEN WILL SOCIETY LISTEN TO CHILDREN?

When I was in senior school and we had an English exam, we had to write a story for our Literature paper. I wrote my true story about how my older brother was sexually abusing me. I told exactly, from my point of view, what was going on at home. I hoped the teacher would realise I was telling her my own story of abuse and that something would be done to help me. The teacher told me what a really good story I had written! But she had no idea that what I wrote was really happening to me. I wanted her to ask me about it, then I would be able to tell her. Some people don't understand this, but you can't just talk about it, you have to be asked – *you have to have permission*. Then, and only then, can you speak.

Something else I've learned from the counselling course is not to beat myself up if things don't go to plan, because I felt I needed to be in control of everything in my life. This is something that comes from the experience of abuse – not to let other people control me because that would make me weak. It's quite exhausting, both mentally and physically, trying to keep control all the time, never being able to ask for help. I've now learned that asking for help is *not* a weakness, it brings comfort to let other people care for me for a while.

I've also learned how to debate on *Nature v. Nurture*, and I still have no solid evidence that either of these is responsible for how we form as human beings. Being from a family of eleven children, two of whom turned into alcoholics and drug addicts, one became a prostitute, featuring in the local paper at the age of fourteen when she was discovered working in a brothel, one was a paedophile, and most of them were thieves and liars – the question has to be asked, how did I end up so different when we were all raised by the same parents? You have to take into account that Mom had been abused by her own father, therefore she was already a victim when she met Dad, and he was very controlling, a drinker, a thief and a liar. Could this outcome of eleven different characters be brought about by nature? It is said that, not only eye colour, height, intelligence and so on, are set at birth, but also properties such as addictive tendencies, anxiety, depression and a whole host of other emotional conditions that were previously thought to be acquired, not inherited.

For me, the argument about *Nature v. Nurture* will never be completely proven because

"Man masters nature not by force but by understanding."
Jacob Bronowski (1908 – 1974)

The counselling course has brought to me three very special friends – Danielle, Ken and Andrea, and I know we will always be in each other's lives because we've shared this journey together all the way. Someone else I have in my life now is Sarah, my learning partner on Level 3 but, as yet, she hasn't pursued the Diploma. All beautiful people on the inside and outside.

The biggest thing I take from the course is that I have learned to find MYSELF. Just me, DAWN. Not the daughter, the sister, the aunt, the friend, the wife, the mother… but the person I choose to be. I've learned that I am in control of my own destiny, I am the driving force and I should 'trust the process', as Cal would say. Another of her sayings is *"How do you eat an elephant? One piece at a time!"* I started eating this elephant in 2010, without realising it at the time. Now I know, I'm three-quarters of the way through it! Thanks to my lovely tutors at Wolverhampton College, Patty and Cal.

My aim is to counsel survivors of abuse and to have group support for them, to let them know they aren't alone. All this is to make sure society sits up and listens, and stops sweeping things under the carpet. Abuse is not an embarrassment or a dirty little secret. Bringing abuse out into the open will help others come forward and help to educate our own children to break the chain of society's ignorance. I now see myself as someone stronger than I've ever been, or even wanted to be, but – most of all – I see myself as the voice to bring about change where it is so badly needed.

Chapter twenty

Life after Dad... and Mom

After Dad died, the stories I heard about the way he had treated Mom made me question who he actually was. I went through being upset, annoyed, disliking him, hating him – all of these emotions because he wasn't the perfect dad I had loved and adored. He was a man who could be violent and controlling, who could treat my poor mom like dirt by having affairs all over the place. The very traits I find appalling in a human being.

The quickest way to destroy my relationship with Dad was to feed me all of these accusations when I re-connected with my family and let them into my own home, where I felt safe and relaxed, let my guard down. That was the worst thing I ever did. It was also the best thing I could have done, because it taught me some valuable lessons.

I was no longer that quiet, controlled little child: I was an adult who had choices. I began to accept that Dad wasn't a perfect man, but Mom loved him unconditionally, and I loved him as my Dad.

When he was gone, my relationship with Mom was strained for a while, and it was certainly tested, but when it comes down to it, no-one can destroy those memories I carried with me, of the dad I adored. After all, he'd had a very different childhood that affected how he grew up and became an adult; he had to take over as head of the family when his father died and his mother wasn't there to care for his siblings. He had to fight to become a man overnight, to be responsible for looking after the children, supplying them with food for their bellies and keeping a roof over their heads. Forced to grow up far too soon... a childhood lost forever, a child stuck...

With Dad gone, it was something unexpected for me to allow a relationship to build with Mom, because – although she was also my parent – I had this idea that she had known about the abuse and yet did nothing to help me, to save me, whereas Dad really didn't know anything about it. If he had, he would certainly have protected me, saved me. The idea of a child stuck...

Our relationship began with me as her carer. After all she was frail, in grief, not in good health, and I was – am – a caring person. As the years ticked by, she became the Mom I could talk to, have conversations with, and share my children with. She was a wonderful Nan to them. I began to see the vulnerable side of this woman, the loving side, her guard slipping. I began to see ME.

I realised then, from the talks we had about her life, that she was also a child stuck because of abuse, and she spoke of how she felt the abuse she had suffered had affected her. She spoke freely of the love she had for my Dad, and her fierce protection of her children. She began to open the floodgates to her emotions, and I started to let my guard down as she showed her true feelings for me and my abuse. The shift began, from parent to Mom, to best friend. As she became more and more free with her thoughts and memories, I forgave her for not saving me from Derek's abuse. She couldn't have saved me because she couldn't save herself – she was still that abused child, stuck in an adult's body. There we were, both of us, going about our lives, not understanding ourselves, not understanding each other, not understanding that we were stuck. This is what abuse does...

I love Mom and Dad unconditionally – my parents and my best friends.

Abuse makes you build barriers, retreat, not question things. As a child, it makes you form your own ideas, stories, opinions of people, inside your head, especially about adults because you look to them as knowing everything...

If there's one thing I've learned, it is never to presume. Ask the questions and allow yourself to grow – or the abusers have already taken your childhood and they can go on to steal your ability to develop as an independent adult.

Can professionals learn from this? Learn that, when you sit with an adult in front of you, trying to get them to open up about their abuse, this person is in fact a child, stuck inside the adult 'shell'. A child who has been conditioned through fear not to speak out, to speak only when spoken to, and with those threats from their abuser still rolling around in their head, of how the abuser will harm them or their loved ones... because the abuser hears everything, sees everything, knows everyone and anyway, *no-one will ever believe what you say...*

One conclusion I have come to is that nature has an impact on abuse, but it is nurture that allows it to continue, if we don't educate people in how to address it, and just leave it as the elephant in the room, or that taboo subject that we are too embarrassed to address...

Dedication

Writing this book has been a journey that has become part of the bigger, ever-changing journey of my whole life.

When I started writing my story, it was to be my way of explaining my past to my younger son, Harry. My birth family had forced my hand to do something, by spilling their evil tongues to my other son, Charlie, giving him their own version of events before I'd had the chance to talk to him myself. I wasn't going to let them do this a second time – I'd had enough of their manipulating throughout my life.

Putting my story into words became much more than the original intention when I started reading the pages as brought to life by my ghost writer, Maggie. It was then that I thought I could use my story to highlight the failings in the system that should be protecting survivors of abuse like me, and should be encouraging others to speak out. Victims of abuse should be given the strength to help them turn their lives around, to become survivors instead of victims. If I can help others to see that the stigma associated with sexual abuse should be ignored, and that the subject should not be brushed under the carpet, but should be brought out into the open for society to acknowledge and deal with – if I can do that, then I will be achieving what I feel is the only way forward.

There are some people I want to thank.

Sarah, thank you for restoring my faith that there are still real people, kind people, out there since I had my trust and my belief in the human race shattered for a while by the abuse I took from work colleagues. Thank you for your friendship and spirit when I started out on my counselling course.

Danielle, thank you for just being yourself and not trying to be something else. Always kind, caring and non-judgemental. As my learning partner at college, you were always very helpful and informative regarding the lessons I missed through absence. You were my anchor in class.

Andrea, thank you for all your emotional support when I struggled with the essays on the counselling course. You helped me to understand where I needed extra information and you didn't allow your professional status to affect your role as a student counsellor. You have been my emotional strength.

Ken, thank you for always being your crazy, funny, smart, deep self and, above all, for rising above other people's prejudices against you. You kept me laughing throughout with your off-the-wall humour and you have come to know the real me, both in and outside college. You remind me of my Eric and that's why we get along so well – and that's a big compliment, because Eric is everything to me.

Lisa, thank you for your help and support through Harry's illness, and when I suffered my breakdown. Thank you also for not letting my sister come between us. You are a genuinely true friend with a wonderful family who I adore. You are more of a friend to my son, Harry, but I don't mind sharing you with him! *Paul,* thank you for your support when I had my first meeting at work, and for the fun you brought every day. You brought light to what was an otherwise dark time for me. You are full of life, full of fun and you taught me to start living in the real world. You and your mom will always be part of my life.

Angela, thank you for all your strength and support in helping to take care of my mom while I'm busy with college, especially after my 'family' let me down again. Without you, I wouldn't be able to follow my dream to become a counsellor. You are an inspiration to me and you saved my life.

My sons, Harry and Charlie, thank you for all the love and kindness you show to me and to everyone around you. Thank you for growing into beautiful people and not being afraid to express your thoughts and feelings to others. Above all, thank you for making me the proudest mom in the world, knowing I have instilled in you both the quality of being non-judgemental to those around you. Charlie, thank you for supporting me with my college assignments. Harry, thank you for being such a character. I love you both.

My biggest 'thank you' of all is to *my husband, Eric*, for allowing me to grow independently and yet being there in case I fall. Without you, I would only be half the person I am. You are my rock, my soul mate and you rescued me from my old life. I don't say this often enough, Eric – I love you today, tomorrow and always. Without your support and backing, this book would not be.

I would like to thank you all for being genuine, honest people. Please don't change, stay the way you are, because that's what drew me to you in the first place.

Dawn

www.ingramcontent.com/pod-product-compliance
Lightning Source LLC
Chambersburg PA
CBHW071613080526
44588CB00010B/1118